# BASS
# WARS

# NICK TAYLOR

## BASS WARS

## A Story of Fishing Fame and Fortune

McGRAW-HILL BOOK COMPANY

New York  St. Louis  San Francisco  Auckland  Bogotá  Hamburg
London  Madrid  Mexico  Milan  Montreal  New Delhi  Panama
Paris  São Paulo  Singapore  Sydney  Tokyo  Toronto

Portions of the chapter entitled "The Classic" appeared in *Yankee* magazine.

1 2 3 4 5 6 7 8 9 D O C D O C 8 7

ISBN 0-07-062994-3

Library of Congress Cataloging-in-Publication Data

Taylor, Nick.
    Bass wars.
        1. Bass fishing.    2. Tournament fishing.
    I. Title.
SH681.T365   1987        799.1'758        87-13962
ISBN 0-07-062994-3

Book design by Patrice Fodero

*This book is for Clare and John Taylor,*
*my parents and the first writers I knew.*

# Acknowledgments

I wish to thank Gerri and Rick Clunn and Jean and Randy Moseley for their contributions to this book. It could not have been written without their candor and cooperation.

Thanks also to the Bass Anglers Sportsman Society, and especially to Ann Lewis and Harold Sharp, for their consistent and unflagging assistance, and to U.S. BASS for its help at the U.S. Open.

And thanks to the professional tournament fishermen, whose company made this book a pleasure to research and write. May all their dreams come true.

# Contents

# *Introduction*

~~~~~~~~~~~~~~~~~~~~~~~~

On a rainy December day in 1983, I opened the *Atlanta Constitution* to see a story in the sports pages about a fishing tournament. The winner, it said, would make $100,000. That information was startling enough to lure me through the rain to Lake Sidney Lanier, north of Atlanta, to see what this fishing tournament was all about.

There, in the rain and fog, I glimpsed a world I found immediately fascinating. The men returning from the lake had the aura of warriors; their sharp-prowed boats looked like chariots of war; as they emerged from the mist that enveloped the lake, they seemed to be escaping from the smoke of battle. Waiting for them on the shore were families, women and children huddled under umbrellas, as if expecting news of casualties.

At that time I could count my memories of fishing on the fingers of one hand—jug fishing in the waters of Estero Bay, near Fort Myers Beach, Florida, where I grew up; a catfish fin stuck in my big toe; the time I snagged a neighbor's daughter's head with a hook during an errant cast. I had gone bass fishing exactly once, on a farm pond near Atlanta, during an excursion whose purpose was more closely tied to quaffing beer than it was to catching fish. Which was fortunate, because no one caught a thing. Compared to all that, this tournament seemed incredibly romantic.

Then I started learning about the money involved, not only the tournament prizes but the income from endorsements and television shows that some of the fishermen were making, and I began to realize that bass fishing was a bona-fide professional sport. It was still young and undiscovered outside the fishing world, largely because television had not found a way to cover it, but a professional sport nonetheless, with heroes and hungry young men who dreamed of being heroes. Some could be expected to succeed, and others would fail. And that was the basis for a story.

The story could be about any group of people who stake their lives upon a dream, and pursue it through hard times and financial sacrifice. These people happen to be fishermen, but they are people first of all, with the same hopes and fears, triumphs and disappointments that uplift and afflict the lives of all of us. And they are Americans, for it is likely that nowhere else on earth could people make a living, as Rick Clunn likes to put it, "chasing little green fish."

Since that day on Lake Lanier, I have developed a great love of bass fishing and some knowledge of the sport. I have come to admire the bass fishermen, their independence, their skill and single-mindedness, their cordiality and humor. I still am no fisherman myself, but this book is about dreamers and strivers, after all.

# BASS
# WARS

# MegaBucks

Clunn wasn't ignoring the kid. He just didn't know the kid was there. The boy was standing on one foot and then the other, trying to be noticed. He clutched a ballpoint pen and a scrap of paper, and his feet moved in little, urgent steps. He imposed himself toward Clunn; he leaned, he shuffled, he danced, but he was not a precocious boy and he neither spoke nor broke the invisible barrier he regarded as Clunn's privacy. Clunn, slender and tanned leathery, stood there at the lakeside as impassive as a stone. His blue eyes, shadowed by his cap bill, were framed in crow's-feet from squinting in the sun. His shirt-sleeves were rolled down despite the mid-April warmth of central Florida. A crowd of a thousand or so sat in banks of nearby bleachers, laughing and applauding as a man on a raised platform in front of them spoke with an Alabama drawl. People came and went, passing Clunn. Some of them spoke: "Hey, Ricky," causing the boy to look furiously at them, or said, "There's Rick Clunn," to one another. Clunn paid no attention.

The boy waited, but Clunn was lost in thought. He was back out on the glistening blue lake, analyzing, questioning, reviewing his performance. He was searching in his mind for the spot where he had failed. Finally the boy turned and walked away.

1

Clunn's wife had told him the children, above all the children, should never be ignored. "I understand it when you don't talk to me," she said. "They won't understand it. The best thing you can do is go off somewhere by yourself."

Clunn tried to follow his wife's advice and always notice children who wanted autographs, but he had been increasingly distracted. Even Gerri wasn't entirely sure what was going on. In seventeen years of marriage, she had watched him become the greatest bass fisherman alive, and yet she was bewildered and a little frightened by his new obsession. He was reading strange books and listening to strange chants and music that came from the "New Age" sections of record stores. "I'm only a mortal," she said. "A lot of this stuff is lost on me."

Clunn's rivals had reacted with varying degrees of charity. Some, the young ones especially, idolized him as they always had. Others called him "Conehead" Clunn, with a hint of malice in their whispers. Hadn't Clunn already won more money than any other bass fisherman, more than even Roland Martin? What did he want now? Clunn put it simply enough: he wanted to be perfect.

But today perfection had eluded him. That accounted for his blind distraction. The day before, on the third day of the Mega-Bucks bass fishing tournament—the world's first spectator fishing tournament—in Leesburg, Florida, Clunn had put on a charge. It was patented, come-from-behind Clunn, and it had moved him from thirty-ninth to thirteenth in the standings. He had only to move up three more places to be among the ten fishermen who would spend two final days fishing for a grand prize worth $101,000. Even by Clunn's standards, $101,000 was worth fishing for, and it was in such high-stakes contests that Clunn was at his best.

The day before, after Clunn had brought in seven bass that averaged nearly 2 pounds each, he had not been so distracted. After he had weighed them in and watched the satisfying "13-12" flash on the digital display screen, another boy had stood nearby. He was maybe 10 years old, wearing a striped T-shirt, shorts, and grubby sneakers, and Clunn noticed him immediately.

"Can I have your autograph, Mr. Clunn, please, sir?" the boy asked. He held out a small red spiral notebook, the kind that fits in a shirt pocket.

"What's your name?" Clunn asked, taking the notebook.

"Keith."

Clunn found a blank page and wrote, in a squarish, forward-slanting hand,

Keith,

Keep casting.

Rick Clunn

Under his name, Clunn added a two-line drawing of a fish.

Other fans gathered quickly, and pushed forward. A man stepped up and aimed a pocket camera. Clunn straightened to his 6-foot height and pushed his red-and-black cap higher on his forehead. He squinted in the sun, and the crow's-feet fanned out from the corners of his eyes. A smile rounded his face and framed his mouth in dimples. Clunn was four months shy of 40; he looked it in his face and thinning hairline, but he had the youthful intensity of a Little League infielder peering toward home plate. He looked as if he was anticipating something, some signal, like a hard grounder toward third, that would move him into action. The flash winked and Clunn stepped forward and stuck out his hand. The grinning photographer was star-struck. He pumped Clunn's hand and looked silly. "I been watching you. I can't believe I'm meeting you," he said.

"Would you sign this for my daughter Katie?" asked a woman with bouncy brown curls. "That's K-A-T-I-E."

When a second woman approached, her embarrassed husband hung behind. He was tall, with a deep tan and a sun-streaked beard. She was tiny and shy, but apparently determined. "My name's Vickie," she said. "That's my husband, Terry. Ever since you said on television that your wife worked so you could fish, that's all I hear. Can I have your autograph?" She handed him a piece of paper. "He's been after me ever since you said that." Terry hung back, blushing.

Clunn wrote,

Vickie,

Bass wishes.

Rick Clunn

Then he stepped over to Terry and offered his hand. "I'll be looking for you," he said. Terry shook hands gravely, and the couple faded into the crowd that was leaving the lake shore now that the day's fish had all been weighed and released back into the lake.

That evening Clunn had returned to his cottage at the Florida Anglers Resort, in a neighboring town a few miles down the road from Leesburg. Typically, he had chosen to stay well away from most of the other fishermen. He had changed the line on two of his casting reels, retied all his baits, and sharpened their hooks with a small file. The hooks were imported, worm hooks from England and treble hooks from France; Clunn felt they were stiffer, and held a better point.

After tending to his gear, Clunn went out for the simplest dinner he could find, at a Bonanza steak house, where he ordered a well-done hamburger steak, a baked potato, and iced tea. He made one trip to the salad bar. Clunn hated elaborate meals, and he ate less as a tournament went on. He believed his stomach shrank, making him less hungry. Hungry or not, Clunn never ate while he was fishing; it took too much time and concentration.

Over dinner, Clunn talked about seeking perfection. He leaned forward earnestly, and chose his words with care. "This is really getting dangerous," he said, and drew a deep breath. Then he said, "I can control the outcome of a tournament if I really want to do it."

Control the outcome? Win any tournament he chose?

"Yes." He had done it only twice, once coming from thirteenth— "which I'm in now, by the way"—in a single day to win. He could do it, he said, by finding in the untapped power of his mind the secret of positive imagining. By creating a fantasy of winning, he could win. Anyone could do the same thing, but you had to work at it. It took time, solitude, and concentration. He had not had time to do it for this tournament. Time was the problem. Time was the first casualty of fame. His sponsors wanted time. His fans wanted time. His family wanted time. Finally, there wasn't any left.

When he had time, Clunn read exhaustively. He even read while he was driving, dividing his attention between the road and a book propped on the steering wheel of his blue-and-white Ford van. As a student at the University of Texas, where he had majored in aeronautical engineering, then business, then electrical engineering, then computer science before dropping out in his junior year, he had disdained philosophy and literature. Now he was picking his way among the thinking of Socrates and Plato, Henry David Thoreau, Walt Whitman, and Ralph Waldo Emerson. He was reading Indian shamans, Yoga masters, a California positive-thinking disciple named U. S. Andersen, and Richard Bach. Clunn devoured everything that Bach had written. He listened religiously to a taped narration of *Jonathan Livingston Seagull* on his cassette recorder. It helped him prepare for tournaments. Listening to Bach's parable of the perfection-seeking loner, Clunn would find anew the resolution to follow his own instincts, to pursue the vision that he saw and not be swayed by other voices.

Other fishermen thought Clunn was weird. They said of his absorption, "Well, uh....Yeah, he's pretty deep, all right. Yup, pretty deep."

Tired busboys were rattling with the dishes when Clunn left the Bonanza around ten. Later that night, after Clunn was asleep, a weather front sailed across central Florida. It whistled over Leesburg and the weigh-in site at the city's Venetian Gardens park and Lake Harris and the connected lakes of the tournament. The front brought clear, much cooler weather. It transformed the fishing. The next afternoon Clunn led the first flight of boats returning from the lake. He beached his boat on the grassy shore and trudged to the platform that held the scales. A weekday crowd of schoolboys, casually dressed couples, and men in suits with loosened ties craned forward from their bleacher seats and lawn chairs on either side of the weighing stand. There was a murmur of expectation at Clunn's approach. But the bag Clunn carried hung limply with the weight of just one fish.

The master of ceremonies, a tall, solid man wearing a white cowboy hat and a silk neckerchief, stood atop the weighing stand. He wore a massive silver belt buckle and a gold Rolex watch, with leaping bass the centerpiece of each. Clunn's fish was measured and handed up for weighing. Clunn mounted the platform wearily, and heard his obituary read in the MC's Alabama drawl: "Rick is a three-time world champion, the only man to win the BASS Masters Classic on three occasions, and it appears to me, Rick, that you have proven only that you're human."

"Well, I am," Clunn said, bending a long, shirt-sleeve-covered arm to rub his neck. "I'm kind of disappointed, obviously. I would like to thank the people of Leesburg for being such gracious hosts, and I will be back, I promise."

More fishermen were coming in, and a line formed from the shore to the foot of the weighing stand. Clunn made to step down, but the master of ceremonies was not finished with him. "Rick, you don't have to apologize for one fish," he said. "That's only one more than I caught today."

"Well, it was a little tougher today. This front came through, and in Florida, the fronts give me more trouble than anyplace I go. So, like I say, there'll be another day and another tournament and I look forward to coming back for the next one."

"Let's hear it for Rick Clunn, folks."

What went wrong? Clunn wondered, ignoring the applause and walking blindly to the edge of the crowd. Where had he missed his signal, the cue that told him to change lures or move to a new spot? How had his concentration strayed? Or had he just not listened, doing one thing when the water, the wind, the clouds all were telling him to do something else? Outside Clunn's isolated bubble of thought the weigh-in proceeded, and the young boy approached him, gave up, and walked away. The crowd clamored and clapped. The man on the platform touted the winners, the 10 who would fish again tomorrow, winnowed from an original field of over 200. Clunn collected his thirtieth-place check for $4499.50. Taking away the $2200 entry fee and his travel expenses, he had done a little better than break even. He began the long drive home to Texas, towing his fishing boat behind the van.

"That mental thing works both ways," he said, before departing. As Clunn drove, he fretted. He was in a slump, and he was beginning to get worried.

The master of ceremonies was named Ray Scott, but he was known as Mr. Bass in fishing circles. He would rather have seen Clunn stay. Scott needed "name" fishermen like Clunn to help make his tournament a success. Scott, 51, was a garrulous former insurance salesman who had started staging bass tournaments in 1967. He had a boxer's rumpled nose and a crooked grin and a talent for promotion that was a match for P. T. Barnum. Out of his tournaments Scott had cultivated a homegrown empire, organizing a largely rural pastime into the world's largest fishing club, the Bass Anglers Sportsman Society. B.A.S.S.'s membership, which had grown to nearly half a million, provided built-in circulation for a glossy, full-color magazine whose ad revenues were the envy of other outdoor publishers. The one magazine had led, eventually, to six. Scott grew rich, and became an object of both admiration and suspicion.

The tournaments were vital to Scott's enterprise. Through them he had created heroes. Clunn was not the only one, but he was perhaps the greatest. He had won not only the BASS Masters Classic, which Scott was bold to call the world championship of bass fishing, three times; Clunn also had won bass fishing's two other major events, the U.S. Open and the Red Man All-American, sponsored by organizations rival to Scott's. His victories, his mystical sangfroid, his sexy wife and two lovely daughters, his remarkable background and the inspirational, eye-dabbing speeches with which he greeted a big win—for Scott, Rick Clunn was money in the bank. An entire generation of young fishermen had grown up inspired by Clunn's history: how he'd left an office job with Exxon to fish the tournaments, how Gerri had worked in the early, lean years with a daughter to support, how their faith was rewarded with Clunn's back-to-back Classic victories in 1976 and 1977, how he had won again in 1984 with a 75-pound catch that broke his own Classic record. The post office in Montgomery, Texas, population 401, had learned to route letters addressed to "World Champion Fisherman" to Clunn's rural roadside mailbox.

Roland Martin was another hero. Martin, 46, was as different from Clunn as sunshine from moonbeams. He was a sun-bleached blond with high, handsome cheekbones and a smile as dazzling as the noonday glint off an unruffled lake. Martin had a popular TV fishing show and nine B.A.S.S. Angler of the Year titles to his credit, indicating that he had nine times finished the regular B.A.S.S. tournament year with the heaviest catch. Clunn had never done that. Martin had won sixteen B.A.S.S. regular season tournaments. Clunn had won three. But Martin had never won the Classic. It was like winning nine major league pennants without ever winning a World Series. There was debate and, some said, bad blood between Martin and Clunn over which test was more important. Who was the better fisherman?

Scott didn't care one way or the other. Both were box office. But Martin and Clunn both were out of MegaBucks. Five other former Classic winners, bona fide stars of bass fishing, had also been eliminated. Denny Brauer and Gary Klein were going home. Other big names hadn't shown at all: Scott had had trouble pulling the MegaBucks tournament together; by the time he announced it, some of the fishermen had other commitments. The Hemphill gang, for example. Hemphill, Texas, fishermen Larry Nixon and Tommy Martin, both Classic winners, and youngster John Torian, were absent. Damn it all, Scott didn't want to be stuck with a bunch of unknown good old boys and yahoos in his top ten. He was trying to promote a concept.

MegaBucks was the crowning demonstration of Scott's conviction that America was a nation of spectators. He believed that people would watch fishermen fish. He had believed it from the day in 1967 when he invented bass fishing tournaments. Scott was in Jackson, Mississippi, at the time, lolling in his room at the Ramada Inn because it was raining and his insurance calls were finished and it was too miserable to fish. As he watched a basketball game on television, a vision lifted Scott to his feet and made him snap his fingers. His words at that moment were emphatic, if not immortal. "That's it," he shouted. Thus is the moment of revelation recorded in B.A.S.S. annals.

What Scott had envisioned was an honest bass fishing tournament. In 1967, as now, fishing derbies were a popular diversion. You threw some money into a pot, went fishing, and the guy who came in with the biggest fish or heaviest catch won the money. Such events were poorly policed. Men with larceny in their hearts and large bass in their freezers won more than a fair share of fishing derbies, and precious few had gotten caught. Scott's genius was to devise a simple but effective way to head off cheating. He put two fishermen in a boat to monitor each other. Over the years he refined the rules, added safety and conservation measures, and the scandal that tainted some other fishing contests never sullied Scott's.

Scott had big plans for bass fishing, right from the start. After he had staged three tournaments, he published the first issue of

*BASSMASTER* in the spring of 1968 and wrote, "It is my plan that we lift bass fishing up to public par with golf, bowling, and pocket billiards.

"You can't pick up a daily newspaper or flip on the television on Saturday or Sunday without seeing these sportsmen in action."

Television didn't rush to cover Scott's tournaments. How did you cover a contest where the field of play was thousands of acres of water and the competitors climbed into boats and drove out of sight? Now, at last, Scott had an answer, and MegaBucks was it. On Friday, April 11, 1986, he would send ten fishermen into a small lake marked into ten fishing holes. People could see them from the shore. There would be spectators. He knew it. If there were spectators, there would one day soon be television. Live television. A network contract. That was why he needed the big names. Thank God for Orlando Wilson, then. That beady-eyed little sucker had popped up all the way to second. He'd draw a crowd. Wilson had a popular TV fishing show, and signed as many autographs as Clunn and Martin.

Also in the top ten at the end of four days were Charlie Ingram, a tournament regular who'd enjoyed reasonable success, once winning three B.A.S.S. tournaments in the space of six months, and Jack Hains. Hains had won the Classic in 1975, left the circuit to deal with a divorce and money problems, and was just returning. The rest of them were good fishermen, of course, but they weren't stars.

The youngest was Randy Moseley. Moseley was 25, from Lake of the Ozarks, Missouri, in his third year on the B.A.S.S. tournament trail. He'd never won a national tournament, and although he'd come close the year before, he hadn't qualified to fish a Classic. But in the days of practice before the MegaBucks tournament began, Moseley had found what bass fishermen call a honey hole. It was a spot near a lock in a canal between two lakes, and it was technically off-limits, but Moseley didn't take his boat into the off-limits area; he tied to a navigational marker and cast into the spot, and caught bass after bass. When the tournament started, he camped on the spot, hauling in seventeen bass that weighed 44 pounds and 1 ounce to finish third among the qualifiers. For the first time in his fishing career, the spotlight shone on Moseley, and he liked it. Not since his acting days at Southwest Missouri State had the spotlight shone so brightly. He liked it very much indeed.

"Youth is walking tall," Scott intoned when he welcomed Moseley to the weighing stand as he announced the finalists. Moseley bounded up the steps as eager as a puppy. He wore a pair of bright, Hawaiian-style baggy shorts. He had a drawerful of the splashy shorts, in jagged lightning-bolt stripes and flower prints. Most of the fishermen wore shirts emblazoned with logos for boats and motors and lures and sun block cream. Clunn thought the fishermen, himself included, looked like Mexican generals in their logo shirts. Or race car drivers. Otherwise they were conservative dressers. But the bright shorts seemed to go with Moseley's youth, his insouciant charm, his blow-dried shock of light-brown hair. "Not many of the fellows here are in their twenties," Scott pointed out. "It seems to be the prime age is around thirty-three, thirty-four, thirty-five years old."

"Well, I know I've been reading about 'em for a while," Moseley said. The crowd laughed, and he continued eagerly. "Some of these guys are what I guess you could call my heroes. They're all super fishermen. I'm really just glad to be here and to be able to go out again tomorrow and compete with 'em. Here I've grown up and read about 'em and learned from 'em and now maybe I get to use what I've learned from 'em against 'em."

Moseley was typical of a new breed of bass fishermen. They drank little, and rarely smoked or chewed tobacco. They were articulate, trim, and business-minded. Most had spent some time in college, and they recognized that communications skills were as important as fishing ability, for a fisherman who couldn't talk would never be offered seminar or lecture dates, television shows or instructional videos. These young fishermen were in a way Ray Scott's children, for he had created them. Now the various tournament circuits made it possible for Moseley and his friend Randy Blaukat from Missouri, Klein and Rich Tauber from California, Joe Thomas from Ohio, and a host of other young men to perceive bass fishing, once a purely sporting pursuit, as a career. Like sandlot sluggers, slam dunkers from city ghettos, and strapping farm boys who could block and run, as they recognized in themselves both a gift and a passion, they began dreaming of the big leagues. Because of Scott and his imitators, there had been big leagues to dream about.

Moseley stood on the platform and felt that his entire life had been directed toward that moment. He was flat broke and in debt, but opportunity lay before him at long last. He could win a bundle. Jean would look great driving that black Camaro that was part of the prize. She'd look great in that car even with the baby seat. At worst he'd have some walking-around money; he could repay the money he'd borrowed to pay his motel bill after spending his cash on the trip down. And the publicity. Scott was bringing down a flood of it, with the claim that MegaBucks was the first spectator fishing tournament. There were reporters all over the place. There were newspaper stories, and they mentioned Randy Mosley, leaving out the first "e," but Randy didn't care. He'd have plenty of clippings. Sponsors would like that. He might even make *Sports Illustrated*. He'd be on television. *The BASSMASTERS* was planning full coverage on The Nashville Network. Life suddenly was sweet. It was great to be up there talking to Ray Scott, talking about himself, about fishing, accepting Scott's good wishes, feeling the warmth of the sun and the crowd.

"What do you do back in Missouri, Randy?"

"I, uh, have a little fishing guide service. And, uh, I run a bar at night. That's about it. Fish."

A few minutes later, Scott herded the ten finalists to a room at the Venetian Gardens community center. He lined them up behind a long table at the front of the room and invited reporters to ask questions. The fishermen sat there, sunburned noses glowing under their cap brims, exhausted after two days of practice and four days of fishing, with two days still to go. But Moseley was eager to talk. He replied in detail to each question he was asked, and when the questions died, he cleared his throat and said that he had something more to say. "This has been a stone in my craw for years," he said, and then praised bass fishing, the fishing pros, and the tournament sponsors. He spoke of the excitement of the sport, and the obligations of the press. The other fishermen looked at their hands. Orlando Wilson rolled his eyes at Moseley's well-intentioned spiel. Finally Moseley ran out of steam. "I've had that on my mind for about three years," he said. "Thank you very much."

Afterward, everybody was standing around outside the building, drifting off into the evening to tend their tackle and get some supper and sleep, when Moseley was surprised to find Scott standing at his elbow. "Randy, you're nothing but a punk," he said.

"Clean up your act," Scott continued in the same mock-gruff tone of voice. "You're not a clown. Don't look like a clown."

That night, Moseley went out and bought a new pair of shorts. They were shorts like the other fishermen wore, cheek-hugging, conservative, and anonymous, in a solid color. Randy chose a fusty blue. He folded his colorful Hawaiian baggies and put them away.

"Why bass?" somebody had asked Ray Scott at the news conference. "Why not trout?"

"You ever catch a trout?" Scott retorted with the scorn reserved for abject ignorance. Before he could continue Moseley piped in, "Booorrring." "That's right, boring," said Scott, hitching up his long-rise jeans. "I never trusted a fish you had to dress to catch."

If Scott sounded defensive, it was because bass fishermen had long been looked down upon by fishing purists who dressed, he supposed, in waders from Abercrombie & Fitch. Part of the problem is the bass. The black bass is a heavy-bellied tavern brawler, truculent and aggressive, as inclined to strike from irritation as from hunger. He wears camouflage green, and although there is drama in the red flash of gill against his sides, he is without elegance or shimmery beauty. He just looks overweight. Sportswriter Red Smith once wrote that if you hung a watch chain across his avoirdupois, the largemouth bass would look like a Thomas Nast cartoon of vested interests. His appeal is in his unpredictability. Trying to stay one jump ahead of the bass, fishermen had devised endless stratagems for catching him. They had followed him according to the seasons from shallow creek heads to deep water. They tempted him with squishy plastic baits that resembled worms and grubs, wooden stick baits that were jerked along the surface like wounded minnows, diving crankbaits that ran like bait fish under the water and rattled to attract attention. There were hairy jigs to which leathery pork skins were attached. Then there were spinnerbaits and buzz baits that resembled nothing found in nature, but looked more like paper clips and ear bobs appended with feathery gee-gaws. Fishermen pursued the bass with a combination of machinery, speed, technology, and blustery purpose that bore little relation to the sport most people think of as fishing.

"If you want sport, you don't go fishing for largemouth bass to begin with," said Rick Clunn. "Even the best battle rarely lasts more than a minute. You fish for bass because it's the supreme challenge. He's not seasonal. He's in all the states except Alaska. He can live in a multitude of environments—ponds, big lakes, little lakes, rivers....

"Then there's a multitude of conditions that can go into catching this fish. He'll hit for a lot of reasons besides hunger. He's an aggressive predator. You don't have to 'match the hatch' with a perfectly tied fly to catch him when he's feeding. You can trick the fish into hitting. You can infuriate him into hitting. The constant challenge of utilizing all your resources, putting everything together, pattern, technique, the mental competence and intensity—that's why he's such an appealing game fish.

"The fight is not important. That is like death to you and him both. The whole game was up to the point before you set the hook."

The Venetian Gardens parking lot on the morning of April 11 looked like a staging ground for a small invasion. Orlando Wilson arrived in his rented Lincoln Town Car to join shadowy figures moving in the predawn darkness, loading equipment onto identical boats provided for the finalists. The Lincoln was among the perquisites of Wilson's remarkable success. His television show, *Fishin' with Orlando Wilson,* was only part of it. At 38, he owned a television production company that was on the road constantly shooting fishing shows, and earth-moving and construction companies back home in Woodstock, Georgia, north of Atlanta. He produced Roland Martin's fishing show, and one on saltwater fishing. He was planning to build a sporting goods mall, and was preparing to build a 14,000-square-foot house. He wasn't doing badly for a 5-foot, 5-inch munchkin who'd never been to college. You could see in his eyes, which were the color of dark olives, the dancing humor that made him popular, and he wore his gold Rolex watch but never his diamond rings when he was fishing, which helped keep him human. Clunn thought Wilson was "the lousiest well-known fisherman around," but that was another story; Clunn was on his way home, and Wilson was getting ready to go fishing.

One of Wilson's assistants had already loaded his tackle boxes and rods into the boat he'd been assigned. Wilson climbed aboard and sipped a cup of Hardee's coffee.

The rising light revealed the line of sleek boats on their trailers. They looked fast even standing still. Their 18-foot hulls in profile were as sharp and sleek as knife blades. Their fiberglass hulls glittered with embedded flakes of metal. On a plane at 60 miles per hour, only a "V" at the stern was in the water and the boats were as skittish as a motorcycle on a sandy road. Driving one in rough water required strength and concentration. They were propelled by high-performance outboards of 150 horsepower, a limit set by B.A.S.S. for safety reasons. They had carpeted casting decks at the bow and stern, and rolled and pleated bucket seats which absorbed some, but not all, of the pounding the boat took in a chop. Your spine took the rest. Once you got to the fish, the big motor was useless. Then a strange spindly trolling motor, battery-powered for silence, was deployed from the bow in conjunction with sonar depth sounders that could spot fish as little blips and chart the bottom like a map. Onto these chariots of war went tackle boxes as big as steamer trunks, and multiple rods, to be kept on deck at the ready like guns at a shooting party.

Wilson, fastidious in pressed blue jeans, a blue sateen jacket, and new white Reebok tennis shoes, tidied things around the cockpit and shouted greetings at the other finalists. A sanguine curiosity filled the air amid the preparations. Nobody was sure what spectator bass fishing was going to be like, or even if there would be any spectators. You had to figure there would be, in a place where retirement villages and trailer parks dotted the landscape like anthills, and fliers in the rooms at the Holiday Inn announced, "Crab Racing. It's here at last!" Leesburg needed a new industry. Three years of frost had killed the orange groves, and they were canning tennis balls now at the juice factory. The Leesburg Chamber of Commerce believed bass fishing could be that industry. The fishermen agreed that Ray Scott had done a dandy job selling the event. "Scott's a promoter," said Wilson. "You know the difference between a promoter and a con guy, don't you? A con guy gets your money once, but a promoter can get it again and again, and you don't even mind."

A burly black man named James Dawson, called Pooley by everyone who knew him, began shouting orders to drivers in vans and pickup trucks: "C'mon back. C'mon, c'mon. Whoa. OK, you got 'im. Go!" Dawson was a fixture on the B.A.S.S. tournament staff, and he kept up the equipment that was needed at each tournament, from the big blue-and-white trailer that housed the computer hookups to Montgomery to the water-filled troughs that kept the fish alive for weighing. At Dawson's command volunteer workers hitched the boat trailers in a clash of steel and rattling chains. The drivers towed them to a launching ramp at a break in a row of pine trees along the shoreline and shunted the boats into the water. The fishermen, each joined by a note-taking observer from the outdoor press, sat in the boats waiting for instructions. The low boats' raised running lights looked like fireflies floating over the calm water.

The sky lightened. The stars faded. It was chilly, and absolutely clear. Harold Sharp, a gruff, balding former railroad man who'd retired to become the B.A.S.S. tournament director, spoke over an electric bullhorn, ordering the fishermen to line the boats up side by side like horses in a starting gate. *The BASSMASTERS*, the weekly B.A.S.S. television show, wanted drama, and Sharp was willing to provide it. The big Evinrudes coughed and growled and spewed choking white smoke. A helicopter carrying the video crew circled overhead, raining wind and sound. At Sharp's signal, the fishermen shoved their throttles forward and sped across the water in a military "V," slicing the surface of Lake Harris into widening ribbons. The helicopter tilted forward and joined the pursuit. The press men grabbed their hats or lost them. Wilson jockeyed past Sharp's pace boat and into the lead.

The phalanx careened flat out across Lake Harris and under a low concrete highway bridge into a smaller lake. Little Lake Harris was 3 miles long from north to south and about a mile across, and it was to be Scott's proving ground for spectator bass fishing. It had been off-limits until now. Sharp and some helpers had marked the lake into ten sections, or fishing holes, by placing orange stakes around the shoreline; canopied runabouts at anchor marked the centerline of the lake, and there were five holes on each shore. Three of them verged on reed-choked marsh and alligator lairs, but the rest offered good viewing points. The fishermen would fish for an hour, check in with officials on the closest anchored boat, and then rotate clockwise to the next hole until they'd fished them all.

"We really wanted a smaller lake," Sharp said. B.A.S.S. had

originally planned to stage MegaBucks on an 800-acre lake at Disney World, but that plan died over sponsor conflicts—B.A.S.S. and Disney World promoted different outboard motors—and a dearth of entries at the $5000 fee. The entry fee was cut by more than half, to $2200, and the tournament was rescheduled and moved to the Harris chain of lakes. Sharp found Little Lake Harris "a little too big, but each hole was so different I couldn't resist using the whole lake."

Wilson had drawn hole number 8, halfway up the lake's western shore where the lavish homes of Howey in the Hills stood near the water. He scouted the shoreline quickly, and started fishing hard along a row of boat docks interspersed with patches of thick-bladed water grass, called Kissimmee grass, or simply "hay." He had four rods on deck, each with a different lure, and was switching among them when the first spectator appeared. The man, wearing shorts and a sleepy expression, and holding a steaming cup of coffee, stood on the deck outside his kitchen as an Irish setter jumped around his feet. Wilson had just rattled a cast off the tin roof of his boat shed.

"Good mornin'," Wilson called. "I don't think they're awake yet." The man nodded gravely, his arms swagged across his chest.

A moment later Wilson paused in the middle of a retrieve. "Look there," he said, pointing toward the shore. "See those people in the car in that driveway, watching us fish?"

That was the way it began, fitfully, at the first spectator bass fishing tournament. People paused to look without making a commitment. They got out of their cars and then climbed in again and drove on, like they were on their way to work. As the day went on and the fishermen moved from hole to hole around the lake, the spectators grew in number. Elderly couples sat in lawn chairs under spreading live oak trees and looked out over the water. Drivers pulled up near convenient docks and ambled out to watch the fishing. One homeowner pulled her curtains and shooed a fisherman away. But a place called Hide-A-Way Harbor posted a sign on its dock offering free iced tea and coffee to the fishermen, and an emissary made Wilson take one of his caps.

Each spectator had a piece of advice: "Try a red shad worm near the boat dock there." Or, "Throw a Zara Spook up in that corner by those lily pads. Then brace yourself." A big-bellied county deputy drove his patrol boat down a canal after Wilson and called, "Don't forget to spit tobacco juice on your bait."

It was the early afternoon, with the heat rising, when Wilson looked up, startled. He stopped fishing, and cupped a hand to his ear. "Are those guys singing?" he asked, incredulous. "They sound pretty good." Across the water, four men on a pontoon boat were singing barbershop harmonies to the fisherman.

Off the water, the best viewing point was the Highway 19 bridge at the lake's upper end, where the fishermen had come into the lake. The bridge carried heavy traffic, but it had wide shoulders and people could walk safely. Wilson found a small crowd gathered on the roadside at the south end of the bridge. They walked out onto the bridge as he fished among its concrete pilings, and they leaned over the railing to chat. A woman aimed her camera. "One big ol' smile, Orlando," she said. A man in a denim jacket called, "Come on, Orlando, catch a fish."

He caught three by the end of the day. Moseley caught one. A Dalton, Georgia, fisherman named Roger Farmer got lost and fished in the wrong hole, where he caught two bass before Sharp made him move. It was a 5-pound mistake, because under the rules he had to throw them back. But Farmer hauled a 9½-pounder out of a patch of lily pads on the next hole, added three more that together weighed over 6 pounds, and led the field at the end of day one.

Back at the weigh-in, trouble was brewing. Its seeds had been planted the day before, when Sharp was making bathroom arrangements. Sharp was a discreet man. It had occurred to him that fishermen operating for the first time under scrutiny during a ten-hour day might need to relieve themselves discreetly. Normally they just peed over the side of the boat. A couple of municipal employees had hefted one of the portable toilets at the weigh-in site and reported that it could go on a pontoon boat. "But I'd hate to be in it if a wind came up," one of them said.

Something even more frightening came along: a woman knocking at the locker room door. Scott was trying to make bass fishing a major league sport, and now it had a major league problem. Cheryl Gordon, a sportswriter and fishing columnist for *The Orlando Sentinel*, told Sharp she wanted to be a press observer. It hadn't been that easy to find reporters willing to turn out at six in the morning, but Sharp said no. B.A.S.S. had never let women fish its tournaments. It was a matter of the fishermen being able to answer nature's call in privacy, Sharp said, and a trial court judge in New York had upheld the organization in 1978. Gordon replied, "I don't think any of these fishermen are going to let going to the bathroom in front of me stand between them and $100,000." And besides, she added, there was the Porta Potti. Sharp promptly canceled it. The fishermen, he said, couldn't be taking time to run back and forth to a bathroom barge. They'd just have to face away from shore. He was adamant. No women in the boats. The unmentioned side issue was that some fishermen had jealous wives. No telling what could happen when a man and a strange woman got together in an open boat for an entire day. In other tournaments that allowed the sexes to fish together, wives had been known to drag their husbands home if they were paired with a woman.

Gordon, who had plied her trade in NFL and major league baseball locker rooms, fumed a righteous fume. "It's ridiculous," she said. "It just shows they're not ready for professional status."

"Little Woman Spooks a Big-Time Promoter," the *Sentinel*'s Bob Morris headlined his next column. Male reporters from the *Sentinel* and the *St. Petersburg Times* decided in solidarity that they couldn't be observers either. Women's rights, it's safe to say, had not been among the things Scott considered nineteen years before when he set out to bring recognition to bass fishing. He envisioned an organization for "plain, hairy-legged fellows who love to bass-fish more than anything else in the world." Now he was suspended between traditional delicacy and new-style equality. The issue seemed destined to haunt B.A.S.S. Gordon vowed to apply again when MegaBucks came back to town. And the *Sentinel* and the *Leesburg Commercial* threatened a promoter's nightmare, to boycott coverage if she wasn't allowed on board. Scott said he wasn't worried. He said people would be ice-fishing for bass in Little Lake Harris before he'd change that rule.

The fishermen, asked at that day's news conference if they'd mind fishing with a woman, hemmed and hawed. Three of them said they'd be concentrating so hard on fishing that nothing would disturb them. The other seven said they were against it. Moseley

said, "I don't know why, but it just doesn't seem right." He didn't
really care. He thought it might even be fun. Moseley could talk
to anybody. A woman sportswriter would be fun to talk to. But a
guy in his position—just starting out, really—couldn't afford to
make enemies. It didn't take a genius to know what Sharp and
Scott wanted to hear.

The spotlight Moseley had enjoyed at the end of the qualifying
days shifted to Farmer as the new tournament leader. Moseley's
one bass—it had weighed a pound and 12 ounces—and his ninth-
place standing were puny by comparison with Farmer's leading
weight of 15-12. Scott inadvertently returned him to obscurity by
forgetting to mention him as he listed the standings at the end of
the weigh-in. Randy stepped up to the microphone and said, "Did
I say something wrong? You forgot me."

He appeared the next morning wearing a light jacket stitched
with the cursive Ranger Boats logo, jeans over his new shorts, and
moldering Nike tennis shoes. He was cheerful. He felt good just
to be among this elite fraternity of fishermen. Farmer was the leader, but they were all attracting attention and today promised even
more. He'd been on the phone almost every night with his home-
town paper, which was keeping up with its local hero at the tournament. He was optimistic, too. It was not impossible to make up
a 14-pound deficit. Three days before, Arkansas fisherman Jim
Fudoli had weighed-in a 24-pound string. Optimism was in Moseley's character. He was one of those rare persons who could live
one day without worrying about the next or the one just past. Confidence was a necessity in a tournament fisherman, and Moseley
possessed confidence in bucketsful. "It's like any profession, like
doctoring or lawyering," he said. "You have to have the confidence
to go out and compete." Improving only one place would make
him richer. But Moseley was going for the win.

At the beginning it seemed possible. He was on his first hole,
casting a spinnerbait among the water grasses and lily pads near
a boat launching ramp on the lake's eastern shore when he inhaled sharply. "Oh, look at that, will you!" he exclaimed. In the
lily pads to the right of the launch ramp the water surged and
billowed, and a school of bait fish flashed silver in headlong flight.
He cast into their midst. Immediately the rod tip bent, and he set

the hook hard. Five seconds later he dropped a squirming 2-pound bass into the boat's rear live well. "He wanted it, too. He 'bout took my arm off," Moseley said excitedly.

The shiners darted this way and that among the vegetation, riffling the surface of the water. Moseley made several unsuccessful casts and changed rods to tie on a new lure, one with chrome sides and an electric-blue back that resembled the fleeing shiners. It was called a "Rat-L-Trap," for its hollow chamber filled with pellets that rattled to attract attention. A swirl disturbed a patch of grass and Moseley cast toward it. A fish struck the lure and Moseley braced himself, and then stumbled backward when the rod went slack. "Gaw," he muttered with disgust. "He hit it and I missed him. He was big, too."

Up and down a 50-yard stretch of bank, the bass continued their morning feed. Panicked shiners swimming for their lives disturbed the water. In the front of the boat, his foot on the trolling motor controls, Randy pursued their frantic ripples. They blew through waving stands of Kissimmee grass and past some rotted pilings, and then back again while he was still reeling in from the cast before.

"A six-pounder rolled over right in front of me," he said. "That's the one I need." The sun broke over the tree line. It was suddenly warm. In the hills around the lake, you could see orange groves that had been killed by frost: row upon row of dead gray trees. Moseley's eyes were on the water. Shiners kept flashing all around the boat. He fished fast, cast and retrieve, cast and retrieve, switching between the spinnerbait and the Rat-L-Trap.

"I can't believe this," he said. "There's fish feeding all over the place." He made a cast every five or ten seconds, over and over and over. Nothing. "I don't know what to do about this. It's driving me crazy." He kept casting.

By seven o'clock the run was over. The bass went quietly back into their cover, and the shiners retired to mourn their missing. The early sun glinted hard and brassy off the now-calm surface of the water. "A hundred thousand dollars riding on the line, and I can't get 'em to come out of the grass," Moseley moaned. "This is just too much for me to handle."

When Randy was at Southwest Missouri State University, his third college in as many years, he had briefly studied acting. Ac-

Three boys lounged on a long dock beside a sandy swimming beach at hole number 7. One of them was fishing, and as Moseley guided his boat in the direction of the dock, the boy pulled a flapping bass out of the water. It would have gone about 2 pounds. The boy stopped fishing when Moseley neared the dock, and volunteered some information: "John Leech caught one here, and Farmer caught three." Moseley fished without success. As he was leaving the hole for the next one, he said, "That didn't make me feel too good, to see him catch that one and me not be able to catch any."

A crowd of spectators, larger than the previous day's, waited at the bridge. A woman was selling hot dogs and soft drinks from a cart. People called encouragement and took pictures, and that cheered Moseley. A few, carrying cameras and binoculars, followed him from the bridge and crunched through a field of weeds along the shore where he was fishing. Someone on the shore described them as "Moseley's army," and that cheered him even more. "Catch a big one, Randy," a woman called, and he said, "I'm ready when they are."

In the end it was the encounter with the boy, and not the crowd, that colored the remainder of the day. Moments of bright promise went unrequited. Moseley struggled with lost strikes. He landed fish too small to keep. He retrieved plastic worms with telltale tooth marks. Long stretches of boredom and repetitious, dogged casting fell between such moments. He aimed a couple of idle casts at a cottonmouth moccasin sunning itself atop a seawall, and said, "The hardest thing about tournament fishing is keeping a positive attitude no matter what."

Near the end of the day he gunned the boat through towering reeds and tufts of sawgrass into protected backwaters that might harbor "a moose hoss bass. But I really don't care if they're twelve pounds or twelve inches," he added, dropping a weighted plastic worm into weed clumps so thick the bait could hardly find the water. The air was still and close away from the open water. Insects buzzed. A grebe with a yellow-tipped red beak fluffed its feathers behind a cypress tree, and iridescent green dragonflies as delicate as raindrops clung to blades of grass. Moseley worked the bait into a shock of reeds, stiffened, and yanked to find the purple worm bitten off below the hook. Finally, he stood in the bow and shouted, as loud as he could, "Here, fishy, fishy, fishy," and gave a smile of resignation.

He was still working the area close to shore when a houseboat appeared, its stereo booming. The song was an old one, older than Moseley: Sonny James in "Singin' the Blues." He listened, made a face, and said, "I wonder if they've got any Quiet Riot."

Roger Farmer won the thing. Jack Hains was second, and Wilson came in fifth. Moseley finished tenth, almost 3 pounds behind John Leech. That was all established on the lake, Sharp asking each fisherman about his catch so that there would be no surprises at the weigh-in. Sharp brought the fishermen back in formation, the boats pounding and scudding on the waves kicked up by an afternoon breeze. An amazing sight greeted them. Thousands of people—a sheriff's deputy said 3000—lined the shore, overflowing the bleachers, and a spectator flotilla bobbed at anchor. Scott, orchestrating the hullabaloo from the weighing platform, whipped up a round of applause and tooting boat horns as the fishermen reached the Venetian Gardens landing.

"I'm more impressed with this than I was with the fishing, that's for sure," said Moseley, as Wilson, in the next boat, signed autographs.

Moseley was first on the weighing platform and quickly dispensed with. He got no long interview, just a "better luck next time" from Scott before he went on to the next man.

When Farmer was announced the winner, his wife and two daughters climbed the steps onto the platform. First one and then the other child, crying, "Daddy, hold me, too," leaped into the bearded Farmer's weary arms, and somehow there was room for a tearful kiss from their mother. Scott wanted to know how Kathye Farmer felt about the prospect of spending the night with a champion with $101,000 in his pocket. Mrs. Farmer, brown-haired and attractive, replied, "He was a champion before he won this."

Then, as everyone was about to turn toward home, Farmer groped in his pocket and took out two small objects. He held them aloft and his voice turned somber. "My father died when I was at Okeechobee," he said, referring to another tournament. "He always carried a buckeye, and a bent nail, and when he died, I got them." His voice broke, and Farmer paused. The crowd waited, hushed and expectant, as if an eclipse had just begun. Farmer stumbled on. "But I wish he was here, where he could see me." The crowd took a moment to collect itself, many brushing at an eye, and burst into a cheer.

Farmer did not put $101,000 in his pocket, as it turned out. He received a check for $6800, representing the first of ten annual payments on the $63,000 annuity that was the monetary portion of the announced grand prize. The first four winners received annuities instead of lump-sum prizes. B.A.S.S. had purchased the annuities for about two-thirds of their face value, and the selling bank continued to draw interest on the balance as the money was dispersed. The rest of Farmer's $101,000 consisted of the Camaro Moseley had coveted, and a $20,000 bass rig, both provided and outfitted by B.A.S.S.'s corporate sponsors. Of the $667,315 prize pool—the biggest fishing prize ever, Scott contended, and worthy of comparison with the prize offered by the Masters golf tournament being held in Augusta, Georgia, the same week—$307,100 was in the form of cars, boats, and deferred payments.

B.A.S.S. used the merchandise it gave away as well as the annuities to inflate the value of its prize pools. The cars and boats were valued at full retail, but the boats, at least, weren't worth that to the fishermen who won them. Most of the fishermen already had boats, or they wouldn't have been there in the first place. A prize boat could be an albatross. A winner had no way to get it home, and he would more than likely sell it on the spot, under conditions that favored the buyer. Farmer sold his "$20,000" boat for $13,000, and declared the difference as a business loss for taxes.

# *Truman Lake*

Moseley, at least, got his money all at once. He stuffed the check for $7,647.50 into his fat nylon wallet and pointed his loose-jointed GMC van north toward Missouri. As he towed his boat through the greening southern springtime he turned things over in his mind. Even with MegaBucks his career was at a precarious stage. The money he'd won was already spent. He toted it up mentally: $1000 to his father, a small repayment toward the money Otis Moseley had advanced Randy tournament after tournament; $1100 to his sponsors at Beebe Batteries, who helped him with expenses in return for a share of his winnings; $1000 to pay off the four-wheel-drive Jeep Cherokee he used for winter driving; a couple of months' rent payments; a deposit on next year's entry fees; and so on.

The gambler in Moseley wanted to postpone paying the deposits and use the money to dabble in penny stocks. A friend had given him a tip. But more fishermen were entering the invitational tournaments now. More aspiring pros like Moseley joined the circuit every year, and at each tournament lake waited local anglers willing to bet $450 in entry money that they could beat the pros. The touring professionals usually won. They maintained an incredible mastery in the tournament results, even on waters far

from home. But the locals were always a wild-card threat. At worst
they would have a chance to fish with a Rick Clunn or a Roland
Martin for the price of an expensive guide trip, and now and then
one of them would finish high in the standings. With the burgeon-
ing interest in the tournaments, Moseley knew he risked missing
a spot if he didn't send in his down payment the minute next year's
schedule was announced. He had missed a tournament the year
before because his deposit had been tardy, and by missing that
tournament he figured he had missed the Classic. He wouldn't
make that mistake again.

Making the Classic would show people that MegaBucks hadn't
been a fluke, Moseley told himself. The cruel irony was that his
tenth place at MegaBucks, his 44 pounds and 13 ounces of bass,
meant nothing in the Classic race. He was still behind in that race,
back in fifty-first place with a lot of catching up to do. Only the
top thirty-five professionals fished the Classic, as determined by
the pounds and ounces they weighed-in at the six invitational tournaments in the B.A.S.S. season. MegaBucks was a showcase apart
from those qualifying events, only two of which were left now, a
total of five fishing days. Moseley chuckled to himself: the first
was at Truman Lake, Missouri, in Moseley's own backyard.

Moseley had decided that this was the year he had to make the
Classic. Simply making the field brought recognition and prestige.
Winning the Classic could make a fisherman's career. MegaBucks
had brought him a welcome salvo of publicity, but the Classic was
the whole fireworks show. It was the World Series, the Super Bowl,
and the Indianapolis 500 of bass fishing, a bonanza of exposure
that the makers of fishing products craved.

Moseley knew that making the Classic on top of the MegaBucks
finals would give him more leverage to pry money out of sponsors. All he had so far were product deals. Ranger memo-billed
his boat, and Evinrude his motor. Memo-billing was in effect a
product loan. A fisherman got the boat and motor up front and
paid for it at the end of a year, and since he was billed at a discount, he usually made a little money, $800 or $1000, on the deal.
Techsonic Industries discounted Randy's Humminbird depth sounders, and he paid less than retail for his Bagley Silver Thread fishing
line. His All-Star rods were free, and so were many of the lures
he used. He was still using the same battered ABU-Garcia reels

he'd used for years, though now and then he could squeeze a free-bie or a loaner from Jerry Smith, the company's product rep. He wore all his sponsors' logos faithfully on his shirt like a general wore his decorations, and he touted the products he used. But like Joe Thomas said, "You can't eat reels. You have to make a living."

Randy was barely doing that, and since Justin's birth last September the money crunch had gotten worse. He made $15,000 a year taking fishing parties out on Lake of the Ozarks. That was in a good year. Let's face it, he thought, that's what I think I could make in a good year if a good year were to come along. He had all sorts of deals working, too. They were pending, always pending. He had a deal with Randy Blaukat to sell Blaukat's Ultra Tournament Products jigs to a local tackle store. He'd invented a spinner-bait with two oversized spoons; a company was supposed to make it and he was supposed to get something for each one that was sold. He carried extra Beebe batteries along to tournaments, and if he sold one or two he made a little something. But it was hard. It seemed to Randy as if he was always waiting for something to happen.

Jean clerked now and then at the Salt Box, the little antique store on Highway 54 on the way to the lake, but that just made the antiques she wanted less expensive. Randy had seen some relief ahead when Jean's great-aunt Jo left her $35,000, but Jean was saving the money for a house. "Randy's the type that'll just use it," she said. "But I don't want to live like a rat." She wanted a home, a real home of her own, not the rented log cabin–style duplex where they lived upstairs from their landlord in a clearing in the woods.

They were like any young family starting out, dreaming and living for tomorrow. Without a steady income, rich parents, or money set aside, Randy had to scramble to stay on the tournament circuit. Before MegaBucks, he had won $4030 in two years in B.A.S.S. competition. It cost much more than that to compete. Entry fees started at $450. MegaBucks had cost $2200 to enter, although Ranger had spared him that expense; the boat maker often picked up tournament entry fees for fishermen it sponsored. Filling the boat's two 25-gallon tanks cost nearly $50 if you towed the boat into a discount service station. It cost more if you got stuck on the water and had to fill up at a marina, and it was astounding how fast the big outboards burned fuel. A gallon took you 3 miles, and when it was 60 miles to your honey hole and 60 miles back, the economics over three days of practice and three days of tournament fishing strongly favored the gasoline dealer.

Nor was boat fuel the last of the expenses. You had to keep the van in gas and oil, and pray it wouldn't need repairs. Randy's Vandura was 3 years old and already had logged 100,000 miles. Sleeping two to a bed in a motel room saved money, but you still had to eat and even the spaghetti special at Shoney's cost something. Most pros budgeted between $1500 and $2000 to fish a B.A.S.S. tournament. Randy could get by for $1000 if he was careful, but the money had to come from somewhere.

Making the Classic could change everything, Moseley thought again as the miles brought him close to home.

Gerri Clunn could have told Jean Moseley that the pro bass tour wasn't the best way to support a family. Rick made a handsome living now, the kind of living they had talked about all those years before, lying in bed together, the lights out, dreaming but not asleep in the little house they'd built in New Caney north of Houston, Brooke barely 3 months old in her crib in the bedroom down the hall. It had sounded so...so possible, hearing him talking in the dark, the clock ticking quietly, the winter moon lighting a gold patch on the carpet just beneath the window. We'll make $40,000 this first year, he told her. All he had to do was quit his job and fish the tournaments. The windows were closed against the February cold, and she felt the warm, slender length of him beside her, against her right side, and in that cocoon of warmth and darkness it felt, well, it was a little scary but he sounded so sure. He was gone every weekend fishing anyway. Every weekend. They had had their share of fights about it.

And so Rick had quit his job, the $18,000 job that everybody said was the perfect job, lifetime security, a check every week and a pension at the end, the job that made him miserable because it locked him up, hermetically sealed inside the tenth floor of the Exxon building, 50 miles away in downtown Houston. He had worked at Exxon for seven years, since he had dropped out of college, advancing from computer operator to systems analyst. He worked a swing shift. At first she had worked, too, and they never saw each other. Four weeks out of six they worked different shifts. Friday afternoons she'd come home and he'd be off in their ramshackle Plymouth with his bass boat, fishing a club tournament. Then Brooke came and Gerri wasn't working anymore. She was always home in that tract house with the gold carpet and the pressed-wood Mediterranean furniture and Ricky always gone. Resentment simmered in her; in the hierarchy of his affections there was his hobby and then there was his family, bringing up the rear. At least, she thought, if he fished for a living he'd be spending all that time on his career. And lying there, eyes open in the dark, the dreams rising slowly on his quiet, certain words, it sounded so good she wanted to believe him. To help Ricky was to help all three of them, and so she told him, "Yes, go ahead if it will make you happy. Do it. I'll help you as best I can." She knew he had already made up his mind to do it anyway.

One day toward the end of February 1974, Rick drove to work at the Exxon building and gave his two weeks' notice. He came home and told Gerri at the end of the day. Gerri felt like she was at the edge of a tall cliff, losing her balance.

Rick went to his father and said, "Dad, I've quit my job."

Holmes Clunn, an auto parts dealer, said, "What?"

"I've quit my job."

"What are you going to do?"

"I'm going to go on the pro bass circuit."

His father said, "Rick, you'll starve to death."

"No, Dad. I know it's going to be hard, but if I can win the Classic I can make a-hundred-and-fifty, two-hundred thousand dollars a year."

Clunn fished his first B.A.S.S. tournament in March, and won $275.

In April he won $981.50, in May $258, and in June another $275. In June, Gerri returned to her old job at a small oil and gas company, where she kept track of the lease records. She worked part-time at first. She and Rick didn't make enough between them to always pay the bills on time. They scraped along, missing a house note here and there. Juggling the bills engraved a look of determination on Gerri's strong face, handsome with high cheekbones, her mother's blunt nose, and wide-set brown eyes, framed by straight blond hair cut short. One day in August she drove home and found Rick waiting at the door. He had an envelope in his hand. It was a registered letter, The mortgage company was demanding immediate payment for the house. She cried, and he comforted her, held her. The company, however, was not to be comforted.

"It was a good thing they took that house," said Holmes Clunn years later, stroking a forehead full of wrinkles with a hand that held a Viceroy. "You know why? 'Cause it was in a flood-prone area and the septic tank backed up. You couldn't flush the toilet more'n half the time."

The elder Clunn spoke with the benefit of hindsight. He didn't know about the repossession when it happened. "Rick didn't tell me anything about it, or I could have helped him out," he said, still a bit bewildered. Rick and Gerri and Brooke had moved farther north to a two-bedroom, $105-a-month rental in Montgomery, near Lake Conroe, where Rick worked as a fishing guide between tournaments. Days he wasn't working, he stayed home and took care of Brooke.

All this was part of the legend, now, of course. The Rick Clunn story was well-known. The Leesburg couple, Vickie and Terry, had seen it on *The BASSMASTERS*. Clunn preached giving up security for the pursuit of dreams. His example fueled reckless talk at midnight in the bedrooms of young fishermen: His wife worked so he could fish. They lost their house. But look how it turned out.

By the end of April, south central Missouri has seen the end of winter, but good weather has not arrived to stay. The ice in the ravines has turned to mud, the trees are a delicate green, but change comes quickly and the wind retains a sting. The wind off the Rockies has 750 miles to build before it reaches the western tongue of the Harry S. Truman Reservoir and buffets little joke-name towns like Racket, Coal, and Tightwad along Missouri Highway 7. Where the wind has a distance of the lake to work with, it can pile up rows of vicious, choppy whitecaps. You could see them rolling toward the Sterett Creek Marina near Warsaw in the cold, steely dawn of Monday, April 28.

Up the graveled hill from the marina, fishermen bent over trenchermen's plates piled high with eggs and ham or bacon and fried potatoes in Jim and Jerry's restaurant. The air was fragrant with cooking and coffee. Heat rose from the steam trays to mist the cold windows. The men wore flannel shirts, insulated parkas, and baggy rain suits with suspendered bottoms like bib overalls. They exchanged hearty greetings as they left their tables to heap more food upon their plates from the steaming serving trays. Clunn's breakfast was monkish by comparison. He drank a cup of coffee and ordered one to go.

Low, heavy clouds rolled out of the west as Clunn left the restaurant and climbed into his van. The lake showed gray and ugly at the bottom of the hill. In two days, when the tournament began, the fishermen would launch their boats here. Now, during the pre-tournament practice period, launching was permitted anywhere on the lake a fisherman could reach by boat. Clunn drove south to a public launching point on the Pomme de Terre River, one of four river arms that splayed out from the dam at Warsaw like a jagged whirligig. He launched and headed south up the river, sitting on first one hand and then the other and wishing he'd brought a pair of gloves along.

Truman Lake lies in the northern foothills of the Ozark Mountains, astride the ecotone between the eastern hardwood forests and the central plain. The Osage, South Grand, and Pomme de Terre rivers once wound through spruce forests under looming bluffs. It took the U.S. Army Corps of Engineers twenty-five years to overcome opposition to flooding the river valleys. The floodgates at Truman Dam were closed in October 1979, and so the lake is young. Nearly 9000 acres of standing timber were left in the lake as habitat for fish, and the drowned trees still stand, gradually rotting, along the borders of its inundated rivers. The water loosens and softens their underpinnings until a wave or gust of wind can send them crashing down.

The dead trees formed a sad, majestic corridor that Clunn followed up the river. Their cracked gray bark looked like the skin of ancient elephants, and you felt like you were in some wooden boneyard, or the ruins of an old cathedral. Clunn kept his hand on the throttle and watched the edges of the river, peering from inside the hooded sweatshirt he had snugged down over his cap. Suddenly he swung to the left, broached a line of trees, and slowed to enter the mouth of a small, timber-choked bay called Bell Hollow. Clunn maneuvered among the protruding stumps and trees and began casting a jig toward fallen logs and spots of cover near the shore. His casts were short and precise, as deft as smoke rings. They landed in water that was clay-stained from spring rains.

During practice, the fishermen use their experience and instincts to try to locate spots where fish are congregated. Some approach the three-day practice period haphazardly, without a plan. Clunn practiced as if the tournament already had begun. He worked quickly and methodically, covering the shoreline once but no more. He fished standing up, working the trolling motor with one foot propped upon its handle. Other fishermen could always identify Clunn on the water, because he looked like a stork standing on one leg. "Standing keeps you on top of things," he said. "When I sit down it makes me want to go to sleep."

In the springtime, spawning bass keep to creek heads and backwaters. The river arms of Truman Lake offered many possibilities among their sheltered and secluded coves. Clunn covered a segment of Bell Hollow with each cast, as the hand on a clock moves around the dial. By the end of the day he would have a precise mental picture of where fish had hit his lure, and of the stretches of water where nothing had happened, to which it was no use returning. Eliminating unproductive water is as much a part of practice as finding fish.

Clunn fished without speaking. He had no store of fishermen's yarns, and he was by nature reserved and meditative rather than loquacious. At tournaments he often drew partners who welcomed a chance to fish with him as an opportunity to improve their game; amateur golfers who drew Jack Nicklaus in a pro-am might feel the same. But if Clunn's partners asked too many questions, they'd learn quickly that Clunn liked to focus on his fishing. He would cut them off, saying, "My mind can't concentrate on two things at once." He was not so much rude as consistent. Asked what he and his father talked about when they were fishing, Clunn would say, "We don't."

Clunn liked to concentrate. He was religious about it. He felt that by concentrating hard enough he could reach a higher level of performance. Like an athlete who tries to visualize his performance beforehand as a sort of newsreel to follow in action, he tried to project in his mind an image of what he wanted to do.

But Clunn sought a deeper connection. He tried to get inside the act of fishing, to so immerse himself that he achieved a Zen-like state of perfect integration with the environment in which he worked. He pursued an awareness so encompassing it was primitive rather than advanced. He wanted to supplant reason with intuition, to feel rather than think, to know rather than see. He projected himself beneath the opaque surface of the water and moved, blind and helpless, with the bait.

"You need to go across the bottom, bump over a log, fall down the other side. You've got to become that bait," he said. He sought to sense the reverberations of the coming strike, the terrible jaws of the bass opening, the tug of the vortex as the gills flared in the moment before the fish inhaled the bait.

Clunn had no labels for what he was trying to do. He did not subscribe to the teachings of Zen Buddhism, for example. "This mental thing" was all he called his belief in the perfectability of his intuition. His sources of information were as eclectic and varied as Shirley MacLaine, Richard Bach, and Albert Einstein. But he was completely serious in his effort to find a seamless accord with his task, and he hoped to extend it to all aspects of his life.

A favorite quote was one from Einstein:

> I am truly a "lone traveler" and have never belonged to my country, my home, my friends, or even my immediate family, with my whole heart; in the face of all these ties, I have never lost a sense of distance and a need for solitude—feelings which increase with the years. One becomes sharply aware, but without regret, of the limits of mutual understanding and consonance with other people. No doubt, such a person loses some of his innocence and unconcern; on the other hand, he is largely independent of the opinions, habits and judgments of his fellows and avoids the temptation to build his inner equilibrium upon such insecure foundations.

The wind stilled briefly with the sunrise, and then rose again in susurrations through the new green of the birches and willows on the lake shore. Drowned trees with their feet in the water creaked and groaned. Clunn hooked a 3-pounder on the south side of Bell

Hollow. He eased the hook out and slipped the bass gently back into the water. Moving out of the cove and downstream across the river, he came to a wide indentation on the western shore called Mining Hollow, where he caught another 3-pounder. Removing the hook, he knelt on the casting deck and pretended to work on his tackle while he glanced furtively toward another fisherman visible 70 yards away through the tree trunks. Satisfied that his catch had not been seen, Clunn left the spot and drove upriver. Between fishing stops, he snacked on beef jerky, bananas, or cookies.

At nearly 40, Clunn felt a change approaching in his life. He faced too many distractions. Sponsors clamored for appearances and he had trouble saying no. He was gripped by complacency, which he believed came from winning, six months before, $100,000 in the Red Man All-American at Lake Havasu in Arizona. He'd had trouble concentrating since. His mind was wandering and he could not bring it to bear. He liked to ponder a tournament beforehand, think about the lake and the seasonal pattern that would dictate the location of the fish. Too often he found he had no time to think until he was driving to the tournament. He treasured those hours alone on the road, but they were not enough. He had not won a B.A.S.S. tournament in almost a year. And in the meantime he watched Brooke, nearly 13 now, growing up, and Cortney, his second daughter, close behind, and he knew he did not have much time left to be the kind of father he wanted to be. Clunn had tasted success, but as it controlled him it grew bitter. His efforts to concentrate beyond all distraction were aimed at modulating his success and regaining control over his life. If he could dictate the outcome of his tournaments, he reasoned, he would not have to do so many dog-and-pony shows.

These thoughts were in the back of Clunn's mind as he fished the mud flats and creek mouths of the Pomme de Terre.

Warsaw, Missouri, occupies the high ground between Truman Lake and its downstream companion, Lake of the Ozarks. Since construction of the dam, boating and fishing have supplanted coal mining and farming in the area's economy, and a number of small resort motels cater to the boaters and fishing parties. The B.A.S.S. Missouri Invitational filled every room in Warsaw, and the overflow had to find rooms as far away as Clinton some 30 miles west.

Clunn, preferring solitude, rented a campsite adjoining the Sterett Creek Marina, where he slept at night in the back of his van.

"Are you serious?" said Randy Blaukat, his jaw dropping in disbelief. "He sleeps in his van, as much money as he's got?" Blaukat worshipped Clunn. The 24-year-old from Joplin, Missouri, was in his first year on the B.A.S.S. circuit and, on the strength of a good showing in the season's first tournament on the St. Lawrence River in New York, was in a good position to make the Classic. He was, in fact, four positions ahead of Clunn, in twenty-fourth place. Blaukat was 6 feet, 2 inches tall, gee-whiz earnest, and so shy that it took some time for his tousled black hair and matinee-idol features to register. Moseley, who was naturally out-going, called attention to his regular, obvious good looks, but you didn't notice at first how strikingly handsome Blaukat was. Blaukat and Moseley's other roommate, Gene Pearcy of Joplin, were sitting in their room at the Lake Hill Motel, retying their lures and glancing up frequently at a television set tuned to the Playboy channel. Fishing rods stood against the wall like guns in a rack. Snipped ends of monofilament fishing line littered the floor like gossamer pickup sticks. Clothing cascaded from open suitcases, and festooned door handles and dresser tops.

Blaukat wanted to know everything about Clunn. No snippet of information was too small. He soaked up the details like a young baseball fan memorizing his favorite player's statistics. Clunn had won his first Classic when Blaukat was a 14-year-old schoolboy. Reading about it, Blaukat was inspired to start a bass club at Joplin's Parkwood High School. He modeled his fishing after Clunn's example, and he was surprised to learn that Clunn preferred to fish in silence. "Talking doesn't bother me. I think it helps me think," he said. "Now, some people can study and listen to the radio. I can't do that at all." He spoke with the flat accents of the lower midwest and his memories of studying were fresh. Blaukat was less than a year out of Missouri Southern State College in Joplin, where he had graduated in 1985 with a degree in criminal justice.

His absent roommate, Moseley, was in the motel restaurant with B.A.S.S. publicity director Ann Lewis. Moseley's career remained much on his mind, and he wanted Lewis, who was competent and well-regarded among the fishermen, to tell him how to promote himself. But there the conversation also turned to Clunn. "Rick never does well early in the year," she said. "He doesn't concentrate well because the tournaments aren't important enough. But at the end of the year he starts improving as it gets closer to the Classic." Clunn was known as a money fisherman whose performances seemed to improve as the prize money increased.

As people analyzed him, Clunn sprawled in the back of his van and read *The Magic in Your Mind* in the fading light. The book's blue-tinted cover—a photograph of a girl wearing a headband, staring in what seemed to be an attempt to depict a deep and intense vision—was a parody of California consciousness, but the book was perfectly serious. Clunn had found it in the San Francisco airport. Reading it, he had discovered a garden of thoughts for self-discovery.

Clunn was not a religious man. The Fellowship of Christian Anglers met at every tournament, but Clunn spurned traditional pieties. The hellfire fulminations of a fundamentalist preacher near his grandmother's home in rural eastern Oklahoma had put him off churches. He drew further from the bosom of religion when his sister Linda committed the sin of dancing by taking ballet lessons and was dismissed from a Baptist congregation. Organized churches aside, Clunn believed that within man and nature lay the seeds of a divine creative thought, and he believed that in that thought was the key to many things. He found *The Magic in Your Mind* a provocative assemblage of ideas, and its dog-eared pages were full of notes and underlines. One of the passages he'd marked was a quote from Emerson: "Everything in Nature contains all the powers of Nature. Everything is made of one hidden stuff." The thinking Clunn embraced would have been more at home on a college campus or in a commune than at a bass tournament.

Moseley chose to fish on Truman Lake's Grand River arm during the final day of practice. One thing after another had gone wrong, and he had not had the time on the water he would have liked. As he backed his boat into the water at a public launching ramp, the sky had cleared but the wind still blew briskly from the west. The South Grand flows from west to east, and the lake was wider where Moseley launched than up the Pomme de Terre where Clunn had fished. Moseley steered along the Grand's broad, sweeping curves past white limestone bluffs capped with spruces and hardwoods. After a few minutes he cut left to a tree line that sloped down a meadow into the water, and began casting a spinnerbait among the treetops.

The spruces had been young and luxuriant when the rising water killed them. The stiff gray tangle of their branches made them look like bedraggled hags with crazy hair. Randy kept hanging his lure in the branches.

Like Clunn, Moseley moved from spot to spot looking for a spot where bass were congregated. He changed techniques and baits, switching among the half-dozen rods he kept on deck from the spinnerbait to a jig with a pork-skin "frog" on the hook, to a plastic worm. He fished less intensely and less methodically than Clunn. Another tournament boat drifted nearby, and Moseley paused to chat with its white-haired occupant, a profane old man wearing a camouflage rain suit. "Can't find no damn fish," he complained. "I'd a damn sight rather be hunting turkeys."

"You heard any gobble?" Moseley asked.

"I've tried to call a few times, but didn't get no answer."

"Listen to this," Moseley said. He swallowed twice and sent up a loud series of turkey gobbles from somewhere in his throat. He was proud of his unassisted bird calls, and included ducks, geese, and bobwhite quail in his repertoire. The fellow in the other boat reached into a bib pocket and produced a turkey call, and the two of them gobbled in chorus as the boats drifted.

Storm clouds gathered as Moseley fished in promising timber along Pretty Creek, which entered the Grand River from the north. Moseley strapped his rods to the deck and raced to the Bucksaw Point Marina just in time to avoid a sudden, blinding rainstorm. The restaurant filled up with fishermen and turkey hunters, and the talk turned again to turkeys.

"Dumbest creatures in the world," said Jimmy Crisp, a Missouri angler. Crisp maintained a turkey would stand in the rain with its mouth open until it drowned. "That's dumb," he said.

"No, they're not. They're smart as hell," his fishing partner argued. "If they're dumb, why do you have so much trouble shooting one?"

"'Cause they're too dumb to come when you call 'em," Crisp answered with finality.

Hank Parker, a tall, good-natured pro from North Carolina

who hosted a television outdoor show, ambled in and turned the conversation back to fishing. Parker said he had caught thirty pounds of fish the day before. "But I caught 'em on five different patterns and five different baits," he said with great sadness, shaking his blond head in mock chagrin. "Boys, I don't know what I'm gonna do tomorrow."

The restaurant emptied when the rain stopped. Moseley drove upriver and began casting among trees that lined a dirt road that descended into the water. The wind was blowing up whitecaps all across the muddy lake. They looked like cotton tufts on beige chenile. Moseley struggled with the trolling motor to keep the boat in place as he fished along intersecting tree lines. Soon a boat carrying a lone fisherman approached. It was Blaukat, his nose smeared with sunblock cream. "I can't catch a fish," he said, shaking his head. "I spent two hours on about a hundred-yard stretch of bank. I could not get bit. I've tried everything." He looked around hopefully. "You think there are enough fish in here to do well in the tournament?" he asked.

Moseley had no bonanza to report. It was difficult to keep the boats together in the wind-driven waves, and Blaukat moved off down the lake.

Blaukat was clearly nervous about his chances, and without a clue about where to fish once the tournament started. Moseley said he hoped he drew such a partner. "I'll just kill him," he said, almost crowing with confidence. "Because he'll be saying, 'Oh, I'm not going to catch anything. I'm not doing something right.' He'll say, 'I can't understand what I'm doing wrong.'

"But he'll get bored not catching anything, and he'll be looking over there, or at me to see what I'm doing, and when he gets a strike he'll miss it, because you can't hook 'em if you're not paying attention."

Moseley cast a jig with a pork frog near the foot of a dead tree. He looked back from the bow and grinned. "You just hang in there and if things go right, you can follow me right through the Classic." His rod tip bent and he swung around, at the same time setting the butt of the rod against his belly and pulling back and up. The water swirled where the line disappeared in the water. Then, as quickly as it had bent, the rod went slack and Moseley stumbled backward.

"See what I mean?" he said.

*     *     *

After Tuesday's practice, the fishermen stood around outside a lakeside gymnasium in Warsaw and gabbed until burly Harold Sharp had to herd them inside for the pre-tournament rules meeting. They climbed into the bleachers on opposite sides of the gym floor, chatting and laughing and greeting one another. Their logo shirts and caps carried names like Ranger and Skeeter, Evinrude and Mercury, in colors bright as birthday balloons. Some of the men were accompanied by their wives.

Scott, wearing his trademark cowboy hat, stood under a basketball goal at one end of the floor and entertained the crowd. "You wives, you know when these men are out on the water, there's hardly anybody on the shore but me," he said. For all his innuendo, Scott was a newlywed. The week before, he had married Susan Freeman, the B.A.S.S. creative director; it was the second marriage for them both. Freeman, 40, was a tall blond who matched Scott in wit as well as stature. In her fourteen-year career at B.A.S.S. she had run the direct-mail solicitations that had helped increase B.A.S.S. membership to over 450,000. This week she had stayed home to get her new house in order.

Scott announced that *The BASSMASTERS'* MegaBucks footage would air on The Nashville Network that coming Sunday. Scott was euphoric over the reception accorded the B.A.S.S.-produced show by the cable network's audience. The show had debuted in the fall of 1985 and, despite airing on Sundays against religion in the morning, football in the afternoon, and *60 Minutes* at night, drew ratings indicating it was seen by over a million people each week. *The BASSMASTERS* had even outdrawn a portion of TNN's live broadcast, early in 1986, of the well-publicized Farm Aid concert to benefit financially troubled farmers.

The half-hour show was popular because it condensed three days of tedious fishing into twenty-three minutes of excitement. B.A.S.S. camera crews covered each tournament, tracking the leading fishermen to their far-flung fishing holes, rigging them with wireless microphones, and then waiting for moments of drama. In the process they usually shot over eight hours of videotape. The final product featured slick editing and upbeat music. Between tournaments, profiles and fishing tips of the top pros were part of the fare, sandwiched between tackle ads and Scott in his cowboy hat peddling B.A.S.S. memberships. Responses to B.A.S.S. mail solicitations improved 20 percent after the show went on the air, and the show's popularity proved to Scott that there was a television audience for fishing.

Scott had just one problem with *The BASSMASTERS*, and that was the fishermen. The independent rascals weren't wearing the right clothes. "Reds and whites are not the best colors," he admonished the fishermen sitting in the gym. At least half of them seemed to be wearing one color or the other. "They don't shoot well on TV," Scott explained. Reds "bled" on videotape, meaning they left a trailing image, and whites had "a burnout effect." Scott suggested the fishermen wear "pastel blues, greens, grays, and browns."

Clothing had become an issue once before, at the 1985 Classic, when Scott and B.A.S.S. tried to make the fishermen wear "generic" shirts and caps, without their sponsors' logos. It was a clear attempt to promote B.A.S.S. sponsors at the expense of sponsors who supported the fishermen directly, and the fishermen rebelled. Clunn, for example, threatened to boycott the Classic if he couldn't wear his Skeeter Boats cap at the Ranger-sponsored tournament. The Professional Bass Anglers Association backed the fishermen, and its Los Angeles attorney, Patrick Marley, prepared a lawsuit. But B.A.S.S. backed down.

Cosmetics aside, Scott had great admiration for "his" fishermen. He knew sponsors used them as walking billboards paraded before the sport fishing marketplace. "Let's face it, you're just the pawns of major corporations," he told the finalists at MegaBucks. But Scott saw the men nonetheless as rugged individualists. He idealized them as American archetypes, and viewed them as a patriarch his many sons.

As the pairings were announced for the first day of fishing, the anglers moved outside the gymnasium to meet their fishing partners. They leaned against their trucks, or stood with their heads together, talking quietly and drawing circles on the asphalt with their toes.

"I always wonder why there are no bad fishermen among these guys," Scott said when he followed them outside. "No troublemakers, all easy to get along with, no bad apples. They are all 100 percent glad to see each other, eager to cooperate, work things out, help their partners. They're all different, but they're all just outstanding. I tell you, these men are the flower of American man-hood."

Scott's vision was placid and benign, but the truth was often different. Furious ego wars took place between the partners. The rules required two fishermen to share not only a boat but the decisions that governed the day's fishing. But no one wanted to give up his control. Each wanted to take his boat to his honey hole, and to dictate the approach to the fishing once he got there by running the trolling motor. He preferred to fish "fresh" water from the front of the boat rather than "used" water, that had already seen the forward fisherman's lure, from the back. Fishermen like Clunn, Roland Martin, and Larry Nixon had the clout to insist on their positions if they chose to do so. And others deferred to them in any case. But even lesser pros like Moseley were prone to argue that they and only they should drive the boat and find the fish. Local fishermen frequently found the pros' attitudes overbearing and insufferable.

"If you fish with a 'big-time pro,' you are going to fish his way, out of his boat, no matter what the rules say," one local man complained when Harold Sharp asked fishermen to rate their partners. "I fell prey to the professional's unprofessional tactics," said another. Competing priorities were the issue in the comment of a fisherman who said he was treated "with disrespect and unfairly" by a pro: "He asked me why I wanted to win since he was fishing for the Classic."

The pros differed on which of their number were good partners and which were bad. Martin and Charlie Ingram, who had finished fourth at Megabucks, were said to be particularly insistent on getting their way. Difficulties in resolving two fishermen's competing needs led some of the anglers to complain that they should be allowed to fish alone. But two men to a boat was the cornerstone of the B.A.S.S. ethic. As long as the fishermen monitored each other, there was no need for lie detector tests, which in some tournament organizations were standard for the top finishers.

"Whenever you say everybody has to take a polygraph, it looks like you've got a tournament full of cheaters," Sharp said. He and Scott both recognized that an image of clean-cut good ol' boys in honest *mano a mano* competition played better than a picture of shifty-eyed backsliders strapped to a machine and forced to deny they were crooks before they could collect their prizes. And in fact B.A.S.S. tournaments had been little plagued by cheating, helped in part by rules that penalized fishermen not only for breaking the rules but also for failing to report any violation they detected. Lie detectors were Sharp's court of last resort, used only when a fisherman was accused of cheating. Even then Sharp had to decide a test was warranted.

B.A.S.S. had avoided the specter of cheating, but earlier in the year Scott had been forced to do some explaining of his own over an incident that to a lot of people looked like cheating.

On February 21, after the B.A.S.S. Florida Invitational tournament on Lake Okeechobee, Florida state game officers stopped a tank truck loaded with 360 trophy-size bass. The driver, who had been hired by B.A.S.S., was charged with transporting commercial quantities of game fish without a permit. The lunkers were bound for B.A.S.S. experimental lakes in Alabama. Scott said they were for a study by the Bass Research Foundation, which Scott had founded, into the effects of the "Lake Life Pump," a contraption used to circulate the water in a small lake and keep it from stratifying into oxygen-depleted layers that can kill fish. "This is a project fishermen can understand," Scott said. "It's not one of those egghead studies." But when the matter hit the papers it looked to a lot of Florida fishermen as if Scott was kidnapping their fish for his personal enjoyment.

Scott claimed he'd tried to get a permit but had run out of time. He did have signed papers from the fishermen releasing the fish they'd caught in the tournament to him. The furor seemed to Scott unjust, as if he were being singled out. He groused, "These sons of bitches had to have a picnic. It's the old, 'You've got the king down. Now everybody's got to kick him in the nuts.'"

If Scott felt persecuted by the uproar, he found reason to crow in his vindication. "Jesus once said, 'And the truth shall set you free,' and it always does," he announced in a news release after Florida officials found no intent of wrongdoing. He dismissed the whole affair with a typical rhetorical flourish: "Like Shakespeare would've said, a whole lot of to-do over nothing."

Now, as he looked with a creator's serene indulgence over the fishermen talking in the parking lot outside the gymnasium in

Warsaw, he again was struck with "the quality of these men. They're tough and hardy, but they're such gentlemen," he said. "There's a compassion that flows through them that I don't understand."

Scott much preferred the robe of bass fishing's messiah to the hair shirt of its culprit.

April 30 dawned with streaky clouds over a peach-colored blush in the east. The fishermen and their trailered boats converged on the Sterett Creek Marina and created a traffic jam on the curving road to the wide launch ramp. In the dim light, the pros backed down the ramp with practiced ease, sometimes three at a time, side by side, and bumped the boats off the trailers into the water. Men carrying rods and tackle crossed the parking lot, seeking their day's partner. Now and then a driver would back a riderless boat into the water. After parking, he would return to the water's edge and hitch a ride out to his boat where it floated off the ramp. The air filled with oil smoke and the sound of engines, and running lights glowed atop their slender stalks at the starboard quarters of the boats.

At the bottom of the ramp, two men worked around a scarred and faded 14-foot boat of outmoded design, with a 40-horsepower Evinrude. The pleasure fishermen were like boulders in the swift-moving stream of activity. Somebody yelled at them to turn their truck lights off. As they painstakingly prepared for their day's fishing, one of them looked around him and said, "We were here yesterday, but it was nothing like this." When someone offered that their boat looked like a rose among thorns, he replied, "More like a thorn among roses, you mean."

One by one, the tournament fishermen found their partners and moved to the marina docks to stoke up on coffee and make last-minute preparations.

In the old days, Scott started each day's fishing with a "blast-off," a literal boat race to the fishing spots. That madcap and dangerous tilt among a hundred or more high-powered, fragile boats gave way to safety concerns and a single-file "ooze-off," but it remains an odd thrill to see in the pale first light the small armada assembled on the glassy water, circling slowly like ungainly frigates, most graceful when they're swift.

Dewey Kendrick, a short, thickly built man who was Sharp's

assistant tournament director, began calling out names, and the
boat drivers formed in single file to move through the required
safety and equipment check. Each fisherman wore a life vest.
Clipped to each driver's life vest was a connection to the boat's
controls that, if removed, would stop the motor. The "kill switch"
had a simple but important purpose. It kept the boat from running out of control if the driver was thrown overboard, where he
could be beheaded by a circling boat. In April 1983, Clunn had
been running up the James River in Virginia on his way back to a
weigh-in when he and his partner saw a johnboat circling in the
water. They searched and found a man barely afloat, cut and
bleeding from the head where he had been struck by his propeller. Their rescue effort was one of the few times Sharp lifted the
rule against late check-ins.

The fishermen moving along the dock took colored flags that
would be counted at the end of the day to assure that all the boats
had returned safely. Kenny Johnson, a tall, friendly man from
the B.A.S.S. tournament staff, checked each boat's kill switch and
live wells as the fishermen idled past, and gave his routine send-
off to the fishermen: "Have a good one and a good luck to you."
The boats moved slowly toward open water. Then the pitch of
their engines rose, and they lifted and settled into flat planes at
top speed, dispersing toward the fishing holes. It is still a boat race,
in the end.

During breakfast, after the fishermen had disappeared into the
dawn, Scott received an unsolicited endorsement for his television
show. He was talking about new ways to attract spectators to fishing—"How'd you like to see a hundred-cast tournament?"—when
a man approached and doffed his cap. He thrust the green, flat-
billed cap and a scrapbook at Scott and asked for his autograph
on both. "Your TV show is great," the eager fellow said. "I get up
every Sunday morning and watch it, then I go to church. That
way I can take care of both my religions at once."

The rosy dawn forecast the day badly. Rain descended on Truman
Lake and the surrounding foothills early in the afternoon, and
soon was falling hard. Muddy rivulets ran from the unpaved parking lot and soaked the ground around the big blue-and-white
B.A.S.S. trailer, the raised weighing stand with its digital scales,

and the line of troughs that would keep the fish wet in their bags. The small crowd took the rain lightly at first, disdaining rain gear and lifting hopeful glances toward the sky. But by the time the first flight of contestants nosed their boats against the muddy shore, umbrellas had been raised and hooded slickers donned. Ann Lewis and Bob Cobb, who issued the B.A.S.S. publicity releases, kept their notebooks dry inside large plastic sandwich bags as they took notes.

As miserable as the spectators looked in the steady rain, the fishermen looked worse. Their mile-a-minute race back to the marina had been painful against the pelting raindrops, which stung like needles. Some, like Moseley, kept motorcycle helmets in their boats to wear in case of rain. They slopped up the embankment to the weighing stand, cling-wrapped in their sopping rain gear. The fishermen's normally bright clothing was dull and colorless in the wet, yet the fish seemed brighter, more vividly green as they were brought out to be weighed.

Oklahoma angler Jimmy Houston came to the stand with five bass that weighed 20 pounds and 7 ounces. Houston, a cherub-faced, bandy-legged little man with sun-bleached yellow hair that framed his face in the style of Captain Kangaroo, was known as "the giggling fisherman" because he punctuated his sentences with the sly laugh of a prankster who'd been caught in the act. Houston used a concoction called "Little Stinker," a fish attractant, on his lures.

"You use any of that today?" Scott asked, trying to take people's minds off the water dripping down their necks inside their parkas.

"I had it kind of scrubbed all over my jigs and my spinnerbaits," Houston replied.

"I knew you had something going, sure as the world," Scott said.

"I had some behind my ears, too. You smell it?"

"I sure do," said Scott.

"Good thing you're not a catfish," said Houston, snickering like a schoolboy.

Houston, a fourteen-year veteran of the pro circuit, was in the running for Angler of the Year, but the race at the lower end of the Classic standings pitted younger fishermen against each other. Moseley, Blaukat, B.A.S.S. rookie Rich Tauber, and Joe Thomas from Cincinnati all had a shot at making the Classic. Moseley had drawn the kind of partner he wanted, a tournament first-timer from Illinois named Mike O'Reilly who was content to ride in Moseley's boat and follow Moseley's instincts. Moseley brought four fish to the weigh-in that weighed 10 pounds and 12 ounces, an encouraging boost to his Classic hopes with four fishing days left to qualify.

The fish that would have given Moseley his five-fish limit was the victim of a cedar tree, he said. He had flipped his jig and pork frog into the water through the exposed treetop, and "I pulled the jig out and a three-pounder came out with it in his mouth. But I could see the hook and the hook wasn't in his mouth. It was just the pork.

"He just sat on the top of the water looking at me for a long time. It was probably two or three seconds but it seemed like a long time. Then he let go. It was the craziest thing I ever saw," Moseley said.

"And I set the hook on another one," he added. "I flipped in a bush and he hit real good and he pulled and I pulled back and the line broke, so I sat there for a second and the next thing I know the fish is jumping, the jig's hanging out of his mouth, and he's gone."

Moseley was a hard-luck fisherman. Things like this were always happening to him. "It's driving me nuts," he said, shaking his head in sad admiration of the wily bass.

Clunn's first-day catch at Truman Lake would have satisfied many fishermen, but not Clunn. He was a perfectionist. Four fish weighing 9 pounds and 3 ounces was less than perfect.

"I'm never satisfied," he said over his supper of meat loaf, baked potato, and a salad at The Dock restaurant, as dusk fell over the lake and weigh-in site a hundred yards away. His eyes were red and his face unshaven. "I executed well. I concentrated well. I worked my water well. I made good decisions as far as moving and not moving.

"But I don't like it when I don't catch my limit," he added. He had had a fifth fish in the well, but decided not to risk its falling short of the Missouri 15-inch keeper length. Penalties for bringing in a nonkeeper were severe, 1 pound deducted from the total weight, and not only tournaments but entire seasons had been lost by ounces. Clunn measured the fish several times. Once its tail would brush the 15-inch mark and the next time it would just miss. If the fish tensed while being handled at the weigh-in, it would not measure, and finally Clunn threw it back.

After supper Clunn returned to his campsite and van. He liked to spend the evenings reading. But by the time he tended to his tackle, replacing spent line and retying his lures, it was usually dark. So he would crawl into the bed in the rear of his van and think about tomorrow, trying to visualize the day ahead: where he would be at what time, the cant of the sun, the color of the water, its depth and clarity, the stumps and fallen logs and clumps and fields of water grass, the fall of the bottom away from the shore, the ridgelines and furrows as they appeared underwater in the ghostly murk. Imagining, Clunn would sometimes see events that would actually occur.

Moseley was imagining, too. He lounged on his bed at the Lake Hill Motel with the television turned to the Playboy channel. He said he planned to do "not a damn thing" different on the second day of fishing.

Pearcy had moved elsewhere, but Blaukat fretted and tried to sleep in the fold-out bed in the corner. He and Moseley were different in their tournament behavior. Blaukat liked plenty of sleep, and retired early. Moseley was a night owl who, on the rare nights he stayed in his room, watched television late. The day's fishing had not improved Blaukat's standing in the Classic race, and he was thinking of trying a new spot. "I'm on fish," he said, "but everybody else is on the same ones." He had been in the last of three flights to leave that morning, and when he pulled into his fishing spot he found Houston, Californian Gary Klein, and Mickey Bruce, who entered the tournament in the lead for Angler of the Year, already there, "picking over my hole."

"The fish were there, all right," moaned Blaukat, "but there wasn't any more room to fish for them." Each day, the flights rotated, third to first, first to second, and so on, so that the men in each flight would have a chance to be first at their fishing holes.

Clunn woke at three o'clock on the morning of May 1 and went outside. The stars were brilliant between patches of cloud in the sky over Truman Lake, and he began to think about how he would treat the day if it was clear. Yesterday's rain had been spinnerbait weather; on a clear day the fish were more likely to hit a jig.

By the time the fishermen arrived to launch their boats, the remnants of yesterday's front were streaking down the eastern horizon, and the sky to the west was clear. The air near the earth was still, and the moisture from the lake gave the cool air an extra bite. The fishermen cinched their sweatshirt hoods down around their faces. Some of them wore ski masks.

When they returned that afternoon, there was no need for rain gear. Sunshine emerged through the high, thin clouds and warmed the air. The boats rounded the wooded point of land that sheltered the marina like birds coming home to roost, singly at first and then in gathering clusters.

Clunn came in with three bass that weighed 7 pounds and 14 ounces. The weight flashed on the digital panels above the scales. Scott squinted at the numbers and said, "Rick, you gotta crank up, Bub." Clunn rubbed the back of his neck and looked unhappy, despite a two-day catch of 17 pounds and 1 ounce that put him twenty-first in the tournament, and even improved his Classic standing slightly.

He was more unhappy still when he saw the next day's pairings. The B.A.S.S. computer, programmed to pair men from different states, had put Clunn with John Wilbanks, a Clinton, Missouri, auto worker who was fishing his first B.A.S.S. tournament. There would normally have been no doubt about who would drive in such a pairing, but Wilbanks's eight bass weighed over 29 pounds and he was sitting in fourth place, 10 pounds out of first. Clunn had no sportsmanlike choice but to take a back seat to his partner.

"He's got a shot to win, and he's earned the right to fish his boat and fish his fish. That's the way I look at it," Clunn said. "I don't mind fishing in the back." That was blatantly untrue, for Clunn liked to make his own decisions. "I've also got no qualms about running his boat if he takes to running around like a chicken with his head cut off, because I've got to catch fish too," he said. "But I'm going to try to help him help himself."

Blaukat brought in two bass that weighed 6 pounds and 10 ounces, and moved closer to clinching a spot in the Classic. "If I can get ten pounds tomorrow, it'll all be over," he said, allowing a nervous smile to cross his face. "I'll be tickled to death, and I

won't even have to worry about the last tournament at Chicamauga."

Moseley caught two bass that weighed 6 pounds, and stood
two places behind Clunn in twenty-third. "You would not believe
the fish I lost," he groaned. Three or four fish had come off
Moseley's hook. They had weighed, he guessed, 11 or 12 pounds
easily. He still felt that if he could average 8 pounds a day for
the three fishing days remaining in the season, he could make the
Classic.

Scott's obsession with television disturbed a baby during a lull in
the weigh-in. He had asked the crowd for some applause—it was
useful for *The BASSMASTERS* editors to have a supply of stock
shots of enthusiastic fans to intercut with the tournament leaders
weighing-in—and in the silence that followed the burst of cheers
and clapping, a loud wail rose from the edge of the assemblage.
Heads turned as a bare-shouldered woman in a light-blue
sundress, pushing a baby carriage, walked rapidly away. She was
tall and slender, and moved with long, graceful strides that lifted
her dark hair off her shoulders.

Jean Moseley and 9-month-old Justin were still growing used to
life on the tournament trail. "It's hard sometimes," she said that
evening in the room. Dusk had fallen, and she played with Justin on
the tweed carpet among the snipped-off ends of fishing line. Randy
had taken Randy Blaukat to retrieve his boat, which had broken down
miles up the lake. "He's away so much," she sighed. "He's either at a
tournament, or guiding. And being a new mother,…"

Jean spoke bravely, but there were times when she felt cheat-
ed. Even when Randy was home, one of his favorite pastimes was
talking to his friends on the phone. He thought nothing of calling people all over the map to chat about nothing in particular
while the phone bills mounted. Sometimes Jean felt like saying,
"Hello, Randy. I'm here."

She and Randy had met at Southwest Missouri State, where
she had gone to major in theater arts. She was working backstage
as a makeup artist in *Romeo and Juliet,* when Randy had come in
for his makeup. He was immediately smitten. "Nobody ever went
after me like that," she said. "I didn't like it. We started out slow,
but a year and a half later we got married."

Jean's marriage to Moseley in March of 1985 had not made

everybody in her family happy. Her middle-class St. Louis background was urban and professional. Her mother's father had been a lawyer and a judge. Her father, in aeronautical mapping with the Department of Defense, looked askance at Randy's career, which he considered a hobby and not a way to make a living. Jean defended Randy from her father's sometimes barbed remarks, but she shared her family's concern about money. "I don't want to scrape and scrounge for the rest of my life," she said. "I want to be comfortable."

It had not helped that she was three months pregnant when she and Randy were married, nor that he was in Florida working at a tackle store in the months before the wedding. His return had coincided with a pointed phone call from her father. But that was in the past, and Jean, despite the loneliness of Randy's frequent absences, was "behind him all the way.

"I really admire him for the way he's going after it, the way he wants to be the best," she said. Justin, a beefy baby with chubby arms and legs, scuttled on the floor and grasped everything he could reach.

Moseley returned from the lake in a dark mood. He shied his cap across the room into his fishing rods where they leaned against the wall. Jean looked up in surprise, and Randy seemed embarrassed.

"Aw, I'm just upset I didn't get those fish in the boat today," he said. "I lost one over five pounds, and that made me sick, and there were two that were about three pounds each and one more I guarantee was a keeper. But I'm going to make the Classic," he promised Jean.

Clunn sat where he did not seem to belong, in the passenger's seat next to Wilbanks, as the boats left the next morning for the final day of fishing. He had drawn the hood of his cotton sweatshirt tight around his face, leaving an exposed medallion of flesh from which his eyes peered and his mouth blew vaporous clouds into the cold morning air.

When he returned with Wilbanks to the afternoon weigh-in, Clunn did not go through the line to the scales. He went directly to the parking lot and his waiting boat and van. He would disappoint no autograph-seeking children there. Stowing his tackle for the long drive home to Texas, Clunn could hear Scott's voice over the loudspeaker introducing the fishermen and their catch weights. Wilbanks had done well; his three fish weighed 10 pounds and 14 ounces and his total weight for the three days was an ounce short of 40 pounds. He beat out more well-known fishermen to finish second in the tournament and win $5000. (Texan Larry Nixon was the winner, and received $10,000 and a boat worth $20,000.) Clunn had caught nothing.

Beside the B.A.S.S. trailer, a drained-looking Wilbanks was telling reporters that Clunn "let me do my fishing. He didn't have anything. He stayed behind me all day."

Clunn had let Wilbanks do his fishing, but he had not liked it. He leaned wearily against his boat, cap tilted down against the afternoon sunshine, and told how Wilbanks had vomited twice during the day from nervousness. "His nerves were just shot," Clunn said. "He told me he could never do this for a living."

A long-haired man in his twenties, with a prominent hooked nose and a mustache, walked up and asked Clunn to sign his cap. He hung around for a few minutes, making conversation, and when he left Clunn blurted out, "This is probably the worst year I've ever had. It's starting to bug me. What am I doing mentally to allow this to happen?"

Each time Clunn asked himself this question, the answer was the same. The answer lay within himself, in his ability to concentrate. He blamed a combination of factors. Winning the All-American had "built complacency." His schedule was too crowded, and he found himself unable to think ahead to upcoming tournaments. As a result his practices were unfocused and he failed, as he had at Truman Lake, to locate fish. In *The Magic in Your Mind* he had underlined, "You do not achieve your goal simply by wanting it; you achieve it primarily by thinking about it. Through thinking about it, you grow into an understanding of it, and it is this understanding that delivers the goal in the end." To give himself more time to think, he had decided to cut back on his personal appearance schedule in the coming year, believing he could make up the lost income in better tournament results. Clunn also planned to create a computer record of past tournaments, so that he could recall winning patterns at the touch of a button.

Meanwhile, he had the Classic to consider. Clunn's Truman Lake catch had moved him up in the standings, from twenty-eighth to twenty-sixth. But at 96 pounds and 2 ounces for the year, he would have to catch fish next month in Tennessee. Twice before, he had relied on strong performances at the end of the year to make the Classic. "But I don't like to have to do it," he said. And only two of the four days of fishing at Tennessee's Chicamauga and Nickajack lakes would count toward the all-important Classic.

Clunn was not the only one to return without a fish. Truman Lake was cruel to Moseley, too. He had gotten only one bite all day. The bass had hit his jig, but when Moseley tried to set the hook, his reel had stripped and run off and he had lost the fish. It was, he said, "the most disgusting day of fishing I think I've ever had."

Blaukat did not catch the 10 pounds of bass he said would relieve him from worry at the tournament in Tennessee. The single keeper he weighed-in went 2 pounds, 9 ounces. His tournament weight of 12 pounds, 15 ounces dropped him three places in the Classic standings, and he, like Moseley, could feel the pressure mounting as the final qualifying tournament approached.

Joe Thomas, the golden-haired young Cincinnatian, was another of the fishermen whose last day disappointed him. Thomas had ended day two in sixth place, and had told Scott at the weigh-in he felt the Classic was "within reach. It would be a real dream come true," he said. But on day three he, too, failed to land a fish. Nonetheless, his nearly 28-pound catch vaulted him into the Classic race. He would go to Tennessee just one spot below his friend and traveling partner Rich Tauber, the Californian who was the only tournament pro known to enjoy surfing as a hobby. Tauber had won the rival-sponsored U.S. Open in 1982 and built a career from the victory. But at Truman Lake he had dropped from twenty-ninth to thirty-seventh in the Classic standings.

For the young fishermen who aspired to the Classic, the Tennessee tournament in June offered the torture of uncertainty. And Clunn, who had been there before, was equally uncertain.

# The Super-Invitational

It had gotten so the ambitious young bass fisherman wasn't well-equipped without a press kit. There was so much demand that a chap named George Kramer, formerly of U.S. BASS, had gone into the press kit business with an agency called Faces in Fishing. Moseley had just gotten his. He had paid several hundred dollars for a supply of glossy white portfolios that held his résumé, photo, press clippings, and a sheaf of other materials. On the outside were the words, "Introducing a Pro..." He loaded the press kits into his van.

Early morning fog hung in the trees—full now with summer—that encircled the cleared patch of ground a peaceful distance from the Lake of the Ozarks tourist attractions and resorts. The log house where Randy, Jean, and Justin lived was quiet as Randy packed for the trip to Chattanooga, Tennessee, and the B.A.S.S. Super-Invitational. A friend of Jean's from St. Louis slept without stirring on the living room couch as minutes came and went in blue-lighted digits on the videocassette recorder near her feet. The titles in a small bookshelf against one wall read like a college reading list: *David Copperfield;* Ibsen's *Ghosts* and *A Doll's House; Cyrano de Bergerac.*

Jean lay sleepily in bed wearing a blue robe, with Justin gurgling and playing on the bed beside her. The bedroom was dark and paneled in rough wood. A row of fishing lures hung like drying laundry from a cord stretched between two nails in the wall, and more lures, with their hooks removed, were scattered like loose change atop the dresser.

Randy finished loading the van. Along with two large and two small tackle boxes (his rods were already in their locker in the boat), he packed several pairs of freshly ironed jeans; his bright baggy shorts and his new conservative ones; a supply of new, professionally stitched logo shirts with his name and "Ranger Boats" prominently displayed (the shirts were polyester, so they wouldn't wrinkle in washing where the logos were stitched on); and some fancy cowboy boots. Finally he tossed in a boxful of baseball-style billed caps. A bass fisherman's cap was the most visible expression of his product loyalties, and each of Moseley's had the logo of some tackle or marine manufacturer sewn to the front of the crown. Fishermen with more than one main sponsor were expected to change from one cap to another during photo sessions to keep all their sponsors exposed and happy.

The van finally loaded and his good-byes said to Jean, who was still in bed with Justin, Randy snugged the canvas boat cover down and tied it, and backed the van down against the trailer hitch. The van's rear tires slipped and sprayed gravel as he pulled up the incline to the road.

Moseley planned to meet Randy Blaukat to the south, where Missouri Highway 5 joins U.S. 60 east of Springfield, and drive in tandem with Blaukat to Chattanooga. Since they planned to overfly the tournament lakes, and Blaukat was prone to airsickness, Moseley stopped at Lake of the Ozarks Hospital to see his physician father about some Dramamine.

It was only seven forty-five in the morning, but Otis Moseley had already performed a tonsillectomy and was making his rounds. Randy had him paged, and in a few minutes he strode around the corner into the waiting area and stuck out his hand. He was a man of average height, graying sandy hair, and a light complexion behind his fashionable bifocals. He recounted taking Randy fishing as a boy.

"I had a johnboat, one of those aluminum things, and I had just gotten a new trolling motor," he recalled. "Trolling motors were in the back in those days, or it was on this boat, anyway. So Randy was in the back trying out the trolling motor, steering the boat and fishing at the same time, and I was fishing from the front. I caught one bass all day, but Randy caught, how many was it?"

"Twenty-four or twenty-five," said Randy.

"Ever since then, I don't even bother with a rod. I just take a camera when I fish with him," said Otis Moseley proudly.

But a look of tolerant exasperation crossed his face when he talked about Randy's Classic aspirations. "It's been a long aspiration," Dr. Moseley said. He, like Jean's father, Bob Bradford, found it hard to think of bass fishing as anything but a hobby.

Blaukat's black Nissan four-by-four was waiting at the roadside when Moseley turned onto eastbound U.S. 60 at about ten o'clock. He pulled off the road and stopped behind Blaukat's bass rig, and Blaukat and his friend and fishing buddy Rick Johnson from Joplin walked back to the van, munching oranges. "What say, pro hawger?" Blaukat said. Big bass were called "hawgs." The greeting was a joke between him and Moseley, and now it was a way of relieving the pressure of the upcoming tournament. Blaukat revealed the tension they both felt when he said, "I'll be so glad when this is all over and we've both made the Classic."

"Making the Classic, that's what this trip is all about," Moseley said when he was back on the road, Blaukat following behind. "I'm going to worry about the Classic the first two days. Then I'll worry about winning the tournament."

As the miles rolled away, Moseley revealed a core of doubt beneath the confidence he usually expressed. "I'm really struggling at this," he said. "I've been chasing this dream for three years. If I don't make the Classic this year, I don't know what I'll do. I don't know if I'll be back next year. I just don't have the money."

The small caravan crossed the Mississippi and Ohio rivers near Cairo, Illinois, and the Ozark foothills eased into the undulations of western Kentucky. Everywhere the countryside was rich with new green life. Randy said he had had to plead with Nina Wood at Ranger Boats for help with the Super-Invitational's $1500 entry fee, while Blaukat, it seemed, had sponsors lined up waiting to help him.

"I just don't know how he does that," Moseley said. "I don't know how to get to the right people, the 'yes and no' men." He reckoned his new press kits would help. As he drove, he spun gossamer dreams of the opportunities that the widening exposure of tournament bass fishing would provide. He believed companies outside the marine and tackle fields would soon enter the market for the fishing audience. Randy saw himself handing out samples of Gatorade thirst quencher and Eagle snacks to his fellow fishermen at tournaments. The time was right. He knew somebody who knew somebody who, he thought, could make the connection. It was just a matter of reaching the right person.

"It's got to happen sooner or later," he said. "But if it doesn't happen sooner, it's going to be later."

Moseley was not alone in his thinking. In fact, the Miller Brewing Company had sponsored the Classic in 1973 and 1974. Chevrolet's truck division, which already sponsored television fishing shows like *Fishin' with Orlando Wilson,* continued as a Classic sponsor, and was about to increase its participation with B.A.S.S. tournaments. Clunn was looking for an agent who would not demand a share of his current sponsor contracts to shop him among beer, soft drink, and other types of companies. As bass fishing grew in popularity and exposure, its commercial potential could only encourage striving young fishermen like Moseley.

"I'd be doing all right if I was single, especially after Mega-Bucks," he mused. "But I can't support Jean and Justin on what I'm making. There's no way I can do it."

He seemed to envy his young contemporaries like Blaukat, Tauber, and Thomas, all of whom were single. Blaukat and Thomas saved money by continuing to live with their parents. Was Moseley sorry he was married?

"Yes and no. I've got a good wife and a great little son. But I really didn't have the security to get married when I did. I think I'd like to have had a little more security."

The financial insecurity and long days on the road that often stretched into weeks made domestic happiness and marital longevity an elusive goal for the tournament professional. Paul Johnson, director of research and development for tackle maker Berkley & Company, once estimated the divorce rate among fishermen his company sponsored at 70 percent. Gerri Clunn said that in the years she had followed Rick on the tournament trail she had seen wives of fishermen come and go. "It seems like every year there are two or three new wives to meet" in her small circle alone, she said.

U.S. 60 joined Interstate 24 at Paducah. The caravan turned southeast toward Nashville and Chattanooga, and for many miles the conversation was of exploits with women, lost loves, and one-night stands. Moseley, like most road men, had a supply of jokes that were versions of old standards. He was an avid moviegoer. "I've probably seen every movie ever made," he said, exaggerating by a lot. His taste in films ran toward melodrama and slapstick. He couldn't decide on his favorite movie. Perhaps it was one in James Coburn's "Flint" series, or maybe *Draw*, a TV western that featured Coburn and Kirk Douglas as public enemies and secret allies in a scheme of larceny. He liked *Revenge of the Nerds*, anything starring John Wayne, and the movie of the moment, *Top Gun*. Jessica Lange and Molly Ringwald were among his favorite female stars. Moseley mirrored the popular taste; he liked his emotions excited and his funnybone tickled, and it did not take art to make him happy.

At Nashville, the afternoon shadows stretching long and the air oppressive in the drought that gripped the south, Moseley decided to stop for the night. He consulted his card file full of phone numbers, and soon Moseley's van and Blaukat's truck were rolling, boats in tow, into a warren of modern apartments east of the city. The roads were tracked with red clay from construction sites where more apartments were climbing like fast-growing kudzu up the hills. Moseley rang the bell at one end of a row of apartments that were landscaped with young magnolias growing up against the gray cedar walls. A slight young woman with a gamine's face, wearing a long dress and white, lace-topped anklets, answered the door. Her name was Selena, and she designed and made clothing. Moseley, Blaukat, and Johnson scrubbed off the road dust and pulled on clean blue jeans for a night on the town.

The next morning, as the gentle contours of middle Tennessee gave way to the steeper hills of Appalachia, Blaukat recounted the beginnings of his storybook rookie year on the B.A.S.S. circuit. The season's first tournament had been on the St. Lawrence River in late September. Despite the unfamiliar waters, Blaukat was in the top ten after two days of fishing. On the third day, Hurricane

Gloria lashed the east coast and far away on the St. Lawrence and Lake Ontario, the fishermen felt her fury. By the end of the day, 8- to 10-foot waves were piling up on the lake and placing a fear of God in the contestants.

"I'm normally a pretty fearless driver," Blaukat said with a chuckle. "But, hey, those waves were so high you couldn't see from the bottom of one over the top of the next one if you stood up in the boat, and I wasn't about to stand up. I was sitting in the top ten, I had three fish in the live well, and I didn't care if I weighed them in or not. All I wanted to do was get to the bank."

He did get to shore to weigh his fish, and finished the tournament in nineteenth place. It was a performance he could not duplicate in contests in Georgia, Florida, Texas, and finally at Truman Lake, where he finished seventy-ninth, but it put him on track for the Classic. He had never dropped out of the top thirty-five in the Classic standings.

Blaukat was doing well off the water, too. He and two friends, Bud Hammons and Dan Tibergehin of Joplin, had had a jig mold fabricated the previous summer. It was a three-jig mold of cast-aluminum, into which hot lead was poured to make tear-shaped jig heads in $3/8$-, $1/2$-, and $5/8$-ounce sizes. The mold was an inauspicious item in itself, but later Hammons, out of curiosity, dipped one of the jig heads into the rubbery compound that you find forming an insulated grip on, say, the handles of a pair of pliers. The result was a rubberized jig head on which Blaukat and his partners could offer a lifetime guarantee against chipping. Next they figured out that they could add peppermint and spearmint scent to their ingredients, and produce a nonchipping jig that was pre-scented to mask human odors that repel fish. This seemed to be a transcendent jig, so Blaukat, Hammons, and Tibergehin called themselves Ultra Tournament Products, designed a logo around the American flag, and had some red, white, and blue caps made. They assigned themselves titles and had business cards printed; Blaukat was the public relations and advertising manager. One of his first acts was to name Moseley to the Ultra Tournament Products pro staff.

The operation soon outgrew the garage where the first jig heads were poured, and moved to more spacious quarters in Tibergehin's basement. Bass Pro Shops, a major mail-order retailer, decided to list Ultra jigs, and they were selling at a lively rate. Jigs incorporate a rubber or hair skirt to conceal the hook, and seven Joplinites were working at home tying skirts on Ultra jigs. Two more were employed in packaging. Now Blaukat and company were making 2400 non-chipping, prescented jigs a week, and sending them out as fast as they could make them. Profits went back into the operation.

Blaukat, however, was predisposed to worry. He fretted about fishing, and he fretted about the jig operation. He fretted most of all about the Classic, and declared that failing to make the year-end tournament would place him in dire straights. "I'll be in downtown Joplin at the Soul's Harbor Mission," he said. "I'm really worried. I'm not kidding."

Blaukat feared that sponsors would back away from him if he failed to make the Classic, despite their implied promises of which Moseley was so envious. He had no firm deals, no contracts that he could pull out of a drawer and read for reassurance. Nonetheless, several manufacturers had indicated that if Blaukat were to make the Classic, he could count on monthly retainers. Ranger Boats, Evinrude, Du Pont's Stren line, Fish Formula scent, and Zebco tackle all wanted Blaukat on their teams—if he made the Classic. Blaukat thought their payments would add up to about $25,000 a year, and that Ranger in addition would pay his tournament entry fees.

"If I could win the Classic," Blaukat said, allowing himself to dream a moment, "I see no problem in making $150,000 a year. At my age," he added, with wonder in his voice.

The caravan reached the Chattanooga city limits at noon on Friday, May 30, and followed I-24 along the Tennessee River into town. The tournament would not start until the following Wednesday, and the tournament waters were off-limits for practice until Monday. Moseley and Blaukat originally had planned a Friday meeting with the Choo-Choo Customs van conversion shop in Chattanooga, but the deal they sought had fallen through. They still hoped to fly over Chicamauga and Nickajack lakes before the tournament.

Pro fishermen in recent years had begun using pre-tournament flyovers to supplement the information they received from other sources. Some "pre-fished" tournament lakes extensively, meaning they would move in before the two weeks prior to the tournament during which the waters were off-limits, try to locate fish, and hope they were still there when the tournament began. Some, like Roland Martin, sought out the best local guides and fishermen for their advice, a practice that was prohibited during tournaments but acceptable beforehand. Martin's remarkable success was sometimes credited to the information he gathered in this way. Some, like Clunn, looked up the results of previous tournaments for the locations and patterns that produced the winning strings. Some fishermen were said to resort to the illegal tactic of sending surrogates to fish a lake during the off-limits period, thus gaining more up-to-date knowledge than pre-fishing could provide. All the pros poured over contour maps looking for ridges and furrows and other underwater "structure" where bass were likely to "hold."

Viewing a lake from the air provided information that would take weeks to compile riding around in a boat. Asked at Mega-Bucks about the advantages of an aerial view, Moseley had said, "You can see water color, vegetation. If the water's even semiclear, you can make out depths. You can see a lot of grass patches that you wouldn't know were there. Cruising along at 85 or 90 miles an hour, which is as slow as you can go, you go by a lake pretty fast, but when they get in a turn you can pick up quite a bit of stuff down there, trees, rock piles, just anything that you might think would hold a fish."

Blaukat, as thoroughly modern a fisherman as Moseley, flew the lakes with Moseley whenever he could, despite his airsickness.

Whatever a fisherman might learn from the air went into his calculations with the knowledge he compiled on the water and over the counters of bait and tackle stores. In Chattanooga that meant Lowery's, a bait and tackle emporium fashioned from the shell of an unlamented gas station on Tennessee 58 leading northeast out of town. The Moseley-Blaukat caravan ran a gauntlet of fast-food shops and discount stores and pulled into Lowery's parking lot. Inside, a row of live-bait tanks stood along one wall, and a central cash register was flanked by racks upon racks of crankbaits, spinnerbaits, and jigs and bins crawling with every plastic worm, slug, grub, and salamander that had ever tempted a hungry bass.

Ed Lowery, a heavy, barrel-chested man with a voice raspy from cigarettes, tended store with his son Bill. Ed creaked when he walked, because he had two prosthetic legs replacing the real ones he had lost in an automobile accident. The store was an extension of his obsession with fishing. Tournament fishing, however, did not interest him, since too little fishing was involved.

"I'd want to be sure I stayed until I caught something—three, four days or at least a week," he said that Friday afternoon, as Moseley and Blaukat shopped. "I went fishing once on February 15th and came back the 28th of May." Appreciating as he did the angler's peculiar affliction, Lowery kept long hours during tournaments, opening his store at four in the morning and closing at ten at night. Since the Tennessee River lakes to the north and west of Chattanooga were popular tournament sites—the Super-Invitational was one of seven national tournaments scheduled on them in 1986—Lowery's extended hours were more or less routine.

Ed revealed that the hot bait at a recent tournament—one of the series sponsored by the Hungry Fisherman restaurant chain— was a deep-bodied crankbait called a "Sugar Shad." The version the bass liked best was one that had lost its original paint down to a silver undercoat. The lure company had rushed out a production model to match, and fishermen had stripped Lowery's shelves of it within three days. Moseley bought three in a different color.

Fishermen came and went as Moseley and Blaukat selected from the stock of lures and plastic worms. Almost everyone agreed that Chicamauga was the lake to fish. Nickajack, they said, was dead.

Moseley had planned to fish Nickajack, and the talk, rather than changing his mind, reinforced his determination to fish the downstream lake. He believed he needed to catch 10 pounds a day to leapfrog into the Classic field, and he was convinced that Nickajack held a stock of large smallmouth bass and that he could catch them. Blaukat, needing only to hold his position and therefore able to fish conservatively, disagreed. "If the top pros, who are known for gambling and taking chances, aren't fishing Nickajack, I don't know how Moseley's going to do it," he said.

But while Blaukat pored over contour maps of Chicamauga that night in their motel room, Moseley was out on the town receiving further confirmation of his belief. At a club on the Brainerd Road strip where young Chattanoogans cruised on weekend nights,

Moseley met a man who had been in Lowery's that very afternoon. Soon they were deep in conversation.

"Well, they're catching smallmouths on Nickajack, just like I thought," Moseley reported the next morning. "He told me exactly where they've been catching them."

"On what kind of baits?" Blaukat wanted to know.

"Oh, those were on live bait," Moseley said. "But that doesn't matter. If they're there, I'll catch them."

The Tennessee River descends in twists and turns from the northeast toward Chattanooga, and then flows far to the west through Alabama before it swings north to join the Ohio River. The Tennessee Valley Authority, created during the depression to bring electric power to the rural South through which the river flows, dammed the main stem of the Tennessee to create nine reservoirs between Knoxville, Tennessee, and the river's union with the Ohio at Paducah, Kentucky. Chattanooga lies between the sixth and seventh of those lakes, Nickajack and Chicamauga. The mile-long Chicamauga Dam incorporates a lock for barges hauling coal, wood pulp, grains, and minerals, and boaters moving between the lakes use the lock as well.

It was TVA power lines, along with air currents and canyon walls, that had kept Moseley from making his hoped-for flyover of Nickajack Lake. "They couldn't get me down low enough to see what I needed to see," he reported after calling a charter service on Saturday. He had flown Chicamauga once before, so with Blaukat's consent he decided to scrap the idea and spent the afternoon watching the Indianapolis 500 on television in their room at the Scottish Inn on Lee Highway east of town.

Elsewhere throughout Chattanooga during the weekend, fishermen arrived and took up lodging according to their means and inclinations. Orlando Wilson and his wife, Carolyn, drove up from their home near Atlanta in his Jaguar sedan and checked into the luxurious Choo-Choo Hilton, where newlyweds Ray and Susan Scott were staying. The B.A.S.S. staff and quite a few fishermen registered at the Best Western Airport Inn, where Harold Sharp had arranged for special rates. (Reduced room rates were just one of the concessions B.A.S.S. received in exchange for the economic benefits and media exposure its road show brought to town; local governments and business groups usually put up $10,000 toward B.A.S.S. staff expenses.) Clunn and a few other fishermen stayed outside of town at the Loret Resort Villa and marina, on a stretch of Chicamauga Lake called Harrison Bay.

On Sunday evening the fishermen—they came from twenty-seven states—gathered at a Teamsters Union hall to officially register for the tournament. Reluctant as boys at church, they slowly formed a line to get their registration papers and an array of handouts from manufacturers whose tables were deployed around the walls. Caps, line, hooks, more caps, bandage dispensers, key chains, towels, lures, more line, more hooks, shirt patches, and plastic worms were free for the asking. Pricey items like outboard motor propellers, reels, and various electronic gadgets were laid out for inspection. Fishermen on retainers touted their sponsors' wares to other fishermen.

At the end of the line, short, bandy-legged Jack Hains and slender, bearded Roger Farmer, who had formed a friendship during MegaBucks, painted and repainted lures with a portable spray kit they were peddling. "We're just getting this ready to put out on the market," Hains announced in looping Cajun inflections as the men piled up around his table. "If y'all are interested in knowing more about it, just put your name down here on this little yeller pad." He sprayed a lure and dropped it into an outstretched hand that rose reflexively to take it. "See? Ready to use. It's dry before it hits the water." He grabbed the lure, dipped it in alcohol, and wiped the color off, then sprayed back and forth over a stencil held against its side. "See? Tiger stripes," he said.

Rick Clunn arrived with his father and two daughters. Ann Lewis immediately steered him to one side for a television interview, which took place on a grassy embankment beside the parking lot at the rear of the union hall.

The two girls took the interview in stride. They were used to the attention their father received. Cortney, whose upturned nose was the center of a spray of freckles, turned nonchalant cartwheels in the grass. Brooke, a reedy child on the verge of becoming a willowy young woman, stood to one side looking self-possessed and not at all impatient.

Their grandfather, 67-year-old Holmes Buckner Clunn—"I've

got three last names," he liked to tell new acquaintances—knew many of the fishermen and they knew him. Skinny, wrinkled, and a little stooped, wearing a tan jumpsuit cinch-belted at the waist, he greeted them in a father's proud, proprietary way. He glanced now and then toward Cortney and Brooke, a grandfather taking his baby-sitting seriously. He waved the ever-present Viceroy in one hand when he talked, and the lines in his forehead arched in parabolic symmetry over his raised eyebrows.

Holmes Clunn came from "sawmill and moonshine country" outside McAlester, Oklahoma, where his father ran a country grocery store and his mother was the postmistress in the tiny town of Weathers. After his discharge from the Air Force at the end of World War II, he lived for eighteen months in Fresno, California, the home of his wife Daphene's parents. Rick was born there on July 24, 1946. His father named him Rick, not Richard or Richmond, after a boy who had idolized Holmes Clunn during his seven years as a high school football star in Haileyville, Oklahoma. ("The rules were looser then," he said.)

The family moved to Texas, and settled in La Porte, east of Houston on Galveston Bay, in 1954. Even before that, family vacations had taken the Clunns back to Oklahoma, and Holmes Clunn reckoned that Rick caught his first fish at about age 4. They had enjoyed frequent outings together.

Rick remembered wading the Oklahoma streams in his little-boy briefs behind his father. He had told of splashing down those streams, dodging his father's "Lucky 13" lure, in an emotional speech after his victory in the 1984 Classic, while Holmes Clunn had lain in an undiagnosed coma in a Texas hospital. Rick, hearing his father was near death, had decided to finish the tournament. He had flown to his father's side as soon as it was over. When he'd reached the hospital and told his still-comatose father of the record-breaking victory, Holmes Clunn had suddenly looked up and said, "Rick, where in the hell did you catch all those fish?" Then he'd closed his eyes and lapsed back into his coma.

"Every weekend we were either out hunting, if the season was in, and if it wasn't hunting season we was out every weekend fishing," said the elder Clunn, who had later recovered. "Rick killed so many deer when he was of high school age that he's gotten now where he won't hardly kill a deer." (Clunn still accompanies his father and daughters on hunting trips, but said he has not shot a deer for ten years or more.)

Rick played football, basketball, and baseball in high school. And ran track. Holmes Clunn, despite his football history, "used to work with him all the time at baseball. He was a pretty tough kid. He played second base. I'd hit the ball to him, and if he let the ball get through him, I'd eat him out about it. I said, 'You get in front of that ball if it has to hit you.' I said, 'Stop that ball and don't let it get through you.' And boy, he got where he'd go right down on that knee, and if he didn't catch it, he stopped it anyway."

But Rick's greatest prowess was in fishing. When he was 10, he and his father were on an outing near Marble Falls, Oklahoma. It was a hunting trip, but Rick told his father he'd rather fish than hunt.

"I said, 'OK, Rick, but don't keep any more fish than we can eat tonight.' I got back in that evening from hunting, and he had forty-two bass, fishing with a fly rod. I let them off his stringer. He just couldn't quit fishing."

On Monday, June 1, Moseley launched his boat shortly after dawn just below the Chicamauga Dam. From there the Tennessee River wound southwesterly to the Nickajack dam, near the conjunction of Alabama, Georgia, and Tennessee. It was 22.5 miles from dam to dam as the crow flies, but 46 miles along the river-lake's twists and turns.

A couple slept in sleeping bags in the bed of a small red pickup truck on the rock-strewn flood plain near the launch ramp. The dam loomed imposingly, its huge spillway gates marked with "Dangerous Water" warning signs. Between the dam and a high railway bridge 200 yards downstream, a protruding rock pile marked the entrance to the barge lock across the river at the dam's north end. The rocks extended, submerged, under the railway bridge to a row of huge concrete barge moorings rising from the water like squat totems, sheathed in rusting metal and hung with thick iron mooring rings as big around as one of Ray Scott's Stetsons. Two barges piled with wood chips were tied to the moorings with ropes as thick as a man's wrist. The damp wood chips, steaming in the rising sun, smelled fresh and piney.

Moseley worked down the line of rocks, casting a 7-A Bomber crankbait that had a "coach dog" pattern—small brown markings the shape of cheese curls. He had caught five smallmouths along the same rock line in a B.A.S.S. tournament the year before, and had finished twenty-first. That tournament had been a month earlier, but Moseley did not think the month's difference was important.

"The reason I'm here is to catch a few large smallmouths, and then run downriver and catch some small largemouths," he said, outlining his tournament strategy. He hooked a small smallmouth and threw it back. Down beside the hulking barges, he switched to a new black jig with an arctic fox–hair skirt, and dropped it into the water near one of the mooring piles. His rod tip bent almost immediately. "There's a smallmouth!" he said excitedly, cranking the handle of his spinning reel.

But it was a drum, 8 or 9 pounds, stolid and lethargic. It flapped heavily when Moseley brought it to the surface. Released from the hook, it descended almost as an afterthought. The next bite was another drum. "C'mon, smallmouths, eat," Randy implored.

He moved downriver with the sun rising. Moseley started the big Evinrude to move from one likely spot to another 100 yards away, fishing now along a stretch of riprap overhung with maple trees, now a flat, muddy embankment lined with fallen logs. The few bass he caught were small ones, barely the 12-inch keeper length, if they were that. After two hours he said, "Enough is enough."

Two-and-a-half miles downstream from the dam, South Chicamauga Creek angled into the river from the south. Randy caught a small keeper bass at the creek mouth, and moved upstream, where the glassy surface of the brownish water was dusted with spring pollen. He cast along embankments shaded by beech and locust trees and choked with bamboo thickets. Morning traffic buzzed over a highway bridge.

"I remember it vividly," he said, speaking of the day he and his father had tried out the new trolling motor. "The size of some of the fish I caught that day!" Soon afterward, his brothers had moved from Albuquerque. Fishing did not interest them. His father became more involved with building the Lake of the Ozarks

Hospital, and the time he had to spend alone with Randy dwindled. "It was really the last full day of fishing we had together," Randy said.

Farther down the Tennessee, Chattanooga apartment houses faced the river with lawn chairs on their balconies. Bridges stretched overhead joining downtown Chattanooga with its suburbs to the north. Casting a slender Rapala minnow, Randy coaxed a 15-inch largemouth from a patch of milfoil grass and shook it off the hook. He cast the lure into the grass several times more, but no more fish emerged and he continued downriver.

Lookout Creek joined the Tennessee 11 miles downstream from Chicamauga dam. The creek passed under twin highway bridges and a railway bridge, and widened into a shallow slough where spawning carp splashed in the muddy water. There were many carp, but no bass.

For more than 20 miles downriver, things were much the same. Moseley pointed out spots where he had caught fish, either in last year's tournament or during his several days of unofficial practice. "This is where I caught that six-eleven last year," he said, casting toward a dock behind a small restaurant whose sign, on the road out front, advertised, "Catfish, Steaks." Along a stretch of the shore shaded by overhanging willow trees, he said, "I saw some nice fish in here. They came up and looked at the bait, but they wouldn't take it." When he threw a lure into the water, he reeled it in to find a bass too small to keep or, most often, nothing at all. He tried to find cooler water, but the surface temperature readout on the dashboard gauge kept climbing: 75°F, 76°F, 78°F. At noon the sun was high and cumulus clouds puffed the horizon here and there. White cattle egrets and blue herons fished in the shallows. They and Moseley were the only fishermen around: other tournament boats were absent from the stretch of water he was fishing. Moseley spied some wild geese, and called to them as he had the turkeys at Truman Lake. Since the memory was fresh, he also growled out a mean Indy race car. As the heat rose he stripped from his jeans to the flowered Hawaiian baggies he was wearing underneath, pulled a can of orange drink from the portable cooler, and issued a short burst of conversation.

"There's a lot I need to learn," he said. "How fish relate to structure. Why they're there. Their habits. Migratory patterns.

When a front comes through, fish move, and some people know exactly where the fish are going to be. I can't figure it out yet. One of my biggest problems is I don't talk enough. I don't ask enough questions. I need to get enough confidence in somebody to be able to trust their judgment."

By one-thirty in the afternoon, with a few desultory spinnerbait casts around an old fenceline in what had once been a pasture, Randy decided he had played out his hunches, for that day at least, on Nickajack Lake.

"I thought sure I'd find a concentration of fish somewhere," he said. "But the milfoil isn't grown up enough to hold them." He turned the Ranger's nose upstream and gunned it into a smooth plane that lasted 38 miles and ended back at Chicamauga Dam.

The barges were gone from their moorings, and he began working with the trolling motor up from the mooring piles along the line of submerged rocks toward the dam, casting the Sugar Shad. "I know there are some good smallmouths between here and the dam, if I can just find them," he insisted. He fished to the dam, along the spillway gates, and down the shore to the launch ramp without getting a strike.

It seemed clear that if Moseley fished the lower lake, he would be taking a very long shot indeed. He decided to spend the rest of the afternoon checking out spots in Chicamauga Lake, so he trailered the boat to the other side of the dam and the tournament launch site. Rick Clunn was sitting on the grass near the launching ramp while a Mercury service team worked on the lower unit of his outboard. "Just getting in the water?" Clunn asked pointedly.

"Aw, I've been down on Nickajack, but there's not much going on," Moseley said. "I know there's fish down there, but I couldn't find 'em today. I thought I'd try up here awhile."

Clunn said a local guide fishing Nickajack Dam the day before had reported catching "a boatload of fish."

"Wouldn't you know it," Randy said. "I didn't go down all the way to the dam."

"How far did you go?"

"Down to Bennett Lake (which was really a shallow bay off the main river). About eight miles above the dam."

Clunn shook his head.

*      *      *

On Chicamauga, as he had on Nickajack, Moseley sought familiar territory. Seven miles above Chicamauga Dam, in 2-mile-wide, island-dotted Harrison Bay, he maneuvered his boat through shallow water to a deep hole that had been a farm pond or a small lake before the river was impounded. There, at a spot where he had caught a 6-pounder in pre-practice, he tried to coax a largemouth out of a bush whose upper branches protruded from the water.

Giving it up after twenty minutes, he moved and hooked two small keepers in two casts in a shallow patch of milfoil grass near an old railroad bed that descended through a spotty grove of trees into the water. At a nearby row of boat sheds, where he had earlier caught fish, he was frustrated to find the water had risen and now kept him from squeezing under walkways on either end into the open water behind the sheds. Tournament rules prohibited fishermen from leaving their boats, and he could not reach the area any other way. Motoring back toward the main body of the lake, he noticed two other tournament fishermen practicing on the grassy flat near the old railroad bed.

When he saw Jimmy Spence, a tournament competitor from Georgia who Moseley knew was out of the Classic running, Randy called, "If you run into anything, let me know. I'm six-and-a-half-pounds out of the Classic."

"You need it bad, don't you?" Spence hollered back. "All I can tell you is, use a buzz bait on the timberlines in the early morning." He paused, as if considering whether to mention it. "Have you heard about that old lake bed over there? Because that's where this guy lost a big one last year."

Randy laughed. "I think that was me. I cost myself being in the Classic the second day up there. I lost twelve or fourteen pounds. They just came off. The biggest fish I ever caught flipping, my first fish, eight-and-a-half or nine pounds, just came off."

Spence shook his head of dark hair in sad commiseration. "If I've got anything, I'll let you know," he promised. "I'm so far out of it, it don't matter none to me."

At the end of the day, Moseley knew little more about how to solve his problem than when it had begun. He had confirmed what he already knew—that there were small largemouth bass to be caught in Chicamauga—but he had not confirmed what he suspected about Nickajack. The fish he had caught there were small and scattered. The large smallmouths he believed were there had moved, or were lying low and mocking him. Once the tournament began, he would have to lock through from the starting point on Chicamauga into the lower lake, wasting precious fishing time.

But Moseley still believed the fish were down there. He felt it in his craw. He decided nonetheless to hedge his bets on the one remaining day of practice, staying in Chicamauga and looking for pockets of cool water, where springs were bubbling up and larger fish might still be hiding.

He betrayed his wavering conviction when he said, "What this boy needs to do is draw one of these local guys, who know where a concentration is. With that, and the places I know, like that grass bank where I caught those two, wham blam!—it'll be no trouble getting a limit every day."

But getting a limit did not necessarily mean gaining ground in the Classic standings, so Moseley's problem remained the same. "The problem," he said, "will be getting the size."

"A lot of these younger guys are good mechanical fishermen," said Clunn. "If you put them on a pattern and put them in an area, they're gonna catch fish. Finding fish is what's hard."

On his first day of practice, fishing with his father (silently) on Chicamauga Lake, Clunn had caught sixteen keeper bass. He guessed the best seven-fish limit, when the smaller fish were culled, would have weighed about 16 pounds. Anybody who brought in 16 pounds a day could count on winning the tournament.

A breeze was blowing, and a palpable thickness, more like smoke than mist, lay over the lake and the surrounding low mountains on the morning of the second practice day. The haze softened the high summer green of oaks and maples to a dusty green like that of eucalyptus leaves. Here above the dam the lake was broad. Where Chattanooga had imposed barge moorings, loading chutes, and buildings on the river's edge, and vaulted bridges overhead, Chicamauga's placid vista was broken primarily by homes whose lawns descended to boat docks on the water. Clunn said yesterday's fish had not been concentrated in one or even several holes. He felt he needed more productive fishing holes, and he had eighteen or twenty spots he wanted to try.

Clunn stopped first almost within view of the marina, in open water at the edge of Harrison Bay. Moseley had fished obvious spots close to shore, but Clunn was well away from the closest shoreline, with no obvious structure—trees, brush, or rock piles protruding from the water, for example—anywhere in sight. Before he started fishing, he drove the red-and-silver Skeeter bass boat slowly back and forth, like a dog turning around and around before it is satisfied it is lying down in just the right spot. As he maneuvered the boat, he sighted toward landmarks on shore and kept glancing down at the depth sounder in the boat's dashboard. Above the hard red flashes that indicated the lake bottom, the dial showed a furry red that came and went. That was the milfoil grass, growing up from the bottom in a soupy forest but invisible from the boat as it crisscrossed the surface of the water. Now that the spring spawn was all but over, the bass were moving off their beds into deeper water. Clunn was looking for patchy grass in water 8 to 11 feet deep, the best areas for the baits he liked to fish.

Clunn began fishing methodically. He used a 7-foot Daiwa fiberglass rod, a Daiwa casting reel, and a 7-A Bomber lure, the same shad-shaped crankbait with two treble hooks that Moseley had used early the day before. The flat lip thrusting forward and down under the nose of the lure acted as a hydrofoil, keeping the bait below the surface as it was retrieved. The faster the lure was retrieved, the greater the pressure of the water against the lip and the deeper the bait ran. Thus Clunn could manipulate the bait, varying the speed at which he cranked the reel in order to bring the bait across the top of the grass without fouling the hooks. It was fast—cast and retrieve, cast and retrieve—not the slow, tedious business of working a worm or a jig among submerged brush or timber.

"Most of us are specialists," said Clunn. "We don't fish everything. That's our trouble." His specialty was "anything fast. I don't like to slow down, that's my problem, especially in practice. But in a tournament, if I get strikes, I can slow down and fish a slower bait."

Fast or slow, Clunn never fished idly, even during practice. His computer training had taught him to hate the waste of time and motion. "Every cast should have a purpose," he said. "You should be thinking about every cast you make. Apply it to the structure, the pattern that you're fishing, and do it as efficiently as you can."

He covered the first spot he had chosen in a series of well-aimed casts that produced one strike and one small keeper bass, started the evil-sounding black Mercury motor on the stern, and moved upriver to the next spot. His guide was a rumpled large-scale TVA contour map. He had traced in red and blue the elevation lines marking the edges of the main river channel, where the depth and underwater grass were to his liking. The contours appeared as elongated amoeba shapes, and Clunn had starred the spots he thought most likely.

Now he positioned the boat off a rock bluff that bulged into the far side of the river. The map showed an underwater ledge—the original riverbank—extending from the bluff in a sweeping curve, and Clunn followed the ledge downriver. The breeze tossed the trees along the water's edge.

By 7:10, forty minutes after leaving the marina, Clunn was fishing his third spot. By 7:50, he was on spot number five, and at 8:25, on spot number six, he pulled the morning's second keeper from the lake.

Tournament boats, which had been absent on Nickajack, buzzed by frequently on the broad lake. Clunn tried to stay away from his competitors, and resented it when they stopped and fished too close to him. He was always a recognizable silhouette in his stork pose, and he believed there were fishermen who fished an area simply because he was fishing it. He was fishing his seventh spot when another boat pulled in. "I can't fish with them there," he said. "If you catch anything, you're giving it away." He pulled up the trolling motor and moved on.

The other boat was now obscured, but Clunn was no less sensitive. It was as if he could feel prying eyes across the water. And moving had left his sweep of the area incomplete. Hating to leave any possibility untested, he returned to the spot later in the morning. No sooner had he started fishing than another boat arrived.

"Don't guess I'm meant to work this area," he said, his face grim. He started the motor and headed upriver. "In practice I don't want to show 'em any more than I have to."

On the next spot, he hooked a fish just as a boat was passing. Clunn dropped the tip of his rod and let the line go slack, but he could not shake the fish. "Don't jump, boy," he implored. Then, the boat safely past, he landed the fish and laughed at his paranoia. "Don't have to worry about that one jumping," he said, looking at the catfish flapping in the bottom of the boat.

When he spied Orlando Wilson, Clunn's ill humor returned and he called the fishing show host "the lousiest best-known fisherman I know.

"Don't get me wrong," he added. "He's a good fisherman, but he's not as good as people think he is. You could win a hundred tournaments and not be as well known as a TV star." Clunn, of course, had himself been a TV star, host of *The Southern Outdoorsman* on regional stations in the late 1970s. He was also the star of a video, entitled *Bass Tactics*. It was a smart seller, but had been made from footage shot for other reasons and released without Clunn's consent, and he was suing the 3M Company for royalties and damages. He had chosen not to pursue other television opportunities. Clunn didn't think Wilson—who was one place and 9 ounces ahead of Clunn in the Classic standings—could find fish on his own. "He wouldn't be sitting there if he hadn't seen me here," Clunn said.

It turned out that Clunn was still angry over an interview Wilson had done when Clunn won the Red Man All-American the previous October. The Red Man tournament trail, with weekend tournaments and low entry fees, billed itself as the working man's circuit. Clunn felt Wilson, in the interview, had implied that Clunn, bass fishing's all-time leading money winner, had no business fishing against weekend fishermen, any more than, say, Larry Bird did shooting baskets for money with kids on a city playground. Clunn's point of view was that the All-American's $100,000 prize—the biggest cash award in bass fishing—was no playground pickup game, and he resented Wilson's implication.

Told Clunn felt that way, Wilson acted mystified. "Does he really? I declare," he said.

Later, when Roland Martin drove past and took up station within sight of Clunn, fishing a similar pattern, Clunn said only, "That's rare. I hardly ever see Roland on the water." Clunn was no fan or friend of Martin's, but he respected him as a fisherman, and did not suggest that Martin was trying to usurp his fishing spot.

The sun rose higher and broke through the blanket of haze, changing the lake's leaden countenance to blue. Hawks, weight-

less and aloof, circled the surrounding hills. The gossipy chatter
of smaller birds filled the trees at the water's edge. Clunn took off
the black Skeeter jacket he had worn since leaving the dock that
morning. He was wearing red shorts, a tan, long-sleeved shirt that
protected his arms against the sun, his omnipresent Skeeter cap,
and an unusual pair of red-and-black rubber sandals. Strapped
around the ankle, they were more often worn by rafters on white
water rivers; Clunn had gotten his on a trip he and Gerri made
down the Colorado.

Following his map upriver from fishing hole to fishing hole,
he reached his tenth spot of the day by 9:15. He began alternating among three casting rods, all tied with similar shad-type baits.
They were the 7-A Bomber, a Sugar Shad in a brownish-red color
known as "Tennessee Shad," and a Bagley DB-3. "The difference
is only for the slight variety in the cover," Clunn said. "A spinnerbait would be the ideal thing to go over this milfoil, but you can't
generate enough strikes that way." He was catching occasional
small keepers, and some fish that were too small to measure.

He cast using both hands, drawing the rod back over his right
shoulder and letting fly, ending the cast with the rod tip pointed
directly at the spot where the lure would hit the water. His casts
were long—30 or 40 yards—and accurate. Clunn's slender frame
was not powerful, and he used two hands even when he was using shorter, 5- to 6-foot rods. "I got tired of everybody being able
to outcast me one-handed," he said.

Adding two more rods to his arsenal, he tied one with a plastic
worm and the other with a top-water "chugger," named for its
concave nose that sprayed up water like a bulldozer going through
a mound of dirt when it was retrieved with a lowered rod tip and
a series of jerking wrist motions. Now and then he bit off the
chugger and tied on a long, slender stick bait called a "Hand Danc-
er"; reeled in with the same jerking motion as the chugger, the
stick bait wavered on the surface like a wounded minnow.

Clunn said he preferred fiberglass rods to newer models of
graphite and boron. The Daiwa Apollo 1763 he used was out of
production, and he had had a twin custom-made to match. He
grumbled that the so-called high-tech rods were too sensitive, that
they would literally yank a lure from the fish's mouth as its jaws
were opening in the middle of a strike.

He had taken his complaints to Daiwa, the Japanese tackle manufacturer that paid him as a product consultant, and so far was
frustrated at the results. "I've talked to 'em and talked to 'em, and
I can't get 'em to make the right action. They've made six or ten
versions and ain't none of 'em right. I've sent 'em this one here"—
it was his custom glass rod—"and told 'em, 'Make it like this,' but
they can't do it. The poor guy at Daiwa USA, it's driving him crazy." He was withholding judgment on the latest effort, a graphite
rod with a fiberglass tip.

Clunn was putting the lie to his reputation for silence. He was a
man of strongly held, often unorthodox opinions, and some of
them emerged without prompting. The TVA's Sequoyah nuclear
generating plant lay 13 miles above Chicamauga Dam on a southward-
jutting breast of land known once as Locust Hill. It occupied the
whole of an inside curve in the river, and its massive cooling towers squatted on the land like huge gray truncated tree stumps
above an antiseptic necklace of white riprap at the shoreline.
    "If it was up to me, I'd shut every one of 'em down," he
shouted over the wind as he sped downriver past the plant that
afternoon. "Can you imagine what would happen to this Tennessee River valley if what happened over there"—he was talking
about the accident at the Soviet nuclear plant at Chernobyl—"happened over here? All these people down this river.... It'd make
that over there look like a cherry bomb. I'd just as soon use fire-
wood myself."
    Clunn had the outdoorsman's streak of independence that
showed itself in a suspicion of all big institutions, whether it was
B.A.S.S. trying to expose only its own sponsors at the 1985 Classic, the 3M Company distributing his video, or power companies,
which in his view were withholding viable sources of energy.
"Nobody'll provide solar, because it's free," he said. He also felt
that people played into the hands of the energy producers by becoming too dependent on them. "These people that have $200
and $300 a month energy bills,..." he shook his head. "I have a
pretty big house, and my energy bill is never over $70."
    The sprawling modern edifice that Clunn had built in the hill
country north of Houston was heated and cooled by a bank of
conventional air-conditioner and heat pump units, but he kept it

cool in winter and warm in the oppressive summers. Anybody who wanted to cool off could always go swimming in the lake he'd built out front.

"Gerri and the kids are pretty good about it," he said. "They're not in the house that much anyway." Even when the air conditioner was on, it was set on 80°F or 81°F, not 68°F. Clunn could well afford to pay the power bills, but keeping the temperature near normal was also an act of self-preservation. Clunn believed in staying in touch with his environment. A man could not always duck inside into the air conditioning. On the day that he could not, on the day he was fishing for $50,000 or $100,000, he would need to be able to stand the boiling heat, and then those days without air conditioning would stand him in good stead. He thought of the $50,000 U.S. Open, coming up in July at Lake Mead outside Las Vegas.

For now, Clunn still had the Classic to think about. He was 7 to 9 pounds short of the weight he thought it would take to make the field for the thirteenth time in a row, and he was resisting the urge to fish for just that weight during the two days that counted toward the Classic.

"Even after you've been to and won a Classic," he said, "the tendency in a position like mine is to fish conservatively, for a place in the Classic, rather than to win the tournament."

But Clunn was never satisfied with less than winning. He fished relentlessly all day, moving from one marked spot to another at the edges of the river channel and around the mouths of creeks entering the lake, until he had fished all the areas he had marked. He caught ten small keepers, but no more than two in any single area. His heaviest limit weighed about 6 pounds.

The fishermen gathered at the Teamsters hall for the rules meeting that evening, June 3, and as usual were reluctant to come inside. When they did, they overflowed the chairs and backed up against the concrete block walls and onto folding tables in the corner near the coffee warmer.

Scott rose at the front of the room, hitched up his jeans, and said, "Boys, we've had a lot of firsts lately, but this Super-Invitational is unique. It's a two-part tournament, with a payout after the first two days, and everybody wins, right down to the last-place man. That's right. After day two, we'll announce the Angler of the Year, and the field will be cut to the top 100 fishermen, and they'll go on fishing. Next day we'll cut to the top 50. The winner at the end of Saturday will take away almost $75,000, but the men who go home early won't go empty-handed."

Scott said a lag in entries had cut the purse from the announced $562,000 to $467,800, but that the fishermen who failed to make the cuts would still win money, $665 after Thursday's cut and $798 after Friday's. Some of the fishermen wondered among themselves if it wouldn't have been better to reduce the $1500 entry fee instead. As usual, the top prizes included vehicles and boats that tended to inflate their value; first place, for example, paid $22,166 in cash, but the Ranger rig and customized Chevrolet Suburban that were included in the package were advertised as worth $50,000. The nearly half-a-million-dollar purse was having its desired effect in any case. Local newspapers and broadcast stations were trumpeting the prize as the highest ever offered in a Chattanooga sports event.

For many of the fishermen, the money was relatively unimportant. Four fishermen remained in contention for the prestigious Angler of the Year designation, and the money in recent years had begun to catch up with the prestige. Sponsors like Du Pont's Stren line were offering bonuses of up to $25,000 to their fishermen for finishing the B.A.S.S. regular season in first place. Denny Brauer of Missouri, who entered the Super-Invitational 2 pounds ahead of Georgian Mickey Bruce, said if he could land 20 pounds in the first two days of the tournament, "I can't really care less if I don't get a bite the last two days." Jimmy Houston, the giggling fisherman from Oklahoma, and Texan Larry Nixon were the other two who had a shot at Angler of the Year.

Then there was the seething contention at the lower end, where not only money and prestige but, some felt, careers were at stake. Joe Thomas, who had done so much to improve his standing at Truman Lake, had had an unproductive practice and was worried. Rich Tauber, the California surfer, was more upbeat. Blaukat was beside himself, and Moseley, who arrived at the union hall in a fresh blue shirt, jeans, and cowboy boots that gave him a cocky stride, expressed confidence to match.

Moseley drew Tom Hicks, a Richmond, Virginia, air-conditioning contractor, as his first day's partner. When they went outside to negotiate their fishing plan, Moseley immediately went on the offensive.

"I'll be perfectly honest with you," he said. "I'm six pounds out of the Classic, and I believe there are fish down in Nickajack that'll put me into it."

Hicks was in his forties. He had some gray in his hair and many sponsor logos on his shirt. He had first fished the B.A.S.S. circuit in 1977, had finished twenty-first in the 1983 Classic, and was soft-spoken and deliberate. He appraised Moseley coolly and quietly replied, "Well, I'm four pounds out, and all my fish are in this lake," meaning Chicamauga.

Hicks's was an unassailable position, but Moseley tried once more. "I just know there are some big ones down there."

"We can catch a limit in thirty minutes on my fish," Hicks replied. There was neither doubt nor hesitation in his voice.

Moseley capitulated. "I'll be perfectly happy to go with you wherever…" He paused, thinking. He still could go to Nickajack on Thursday. And if he agreed to go to Hicks's fish tomorrow, he could argue for taking his boat. That would make it easier to divert to Nickajack if Hicks was wrong about his fishing hole. "…as long as I can take my boat."

"I was just getting ready to say the same thing," said Hicks. "My boat's in the water."

"Mine's close." Moseley pulled a coin out of his pocket. A coin toss was a finesse, meant to end discussion. Before Hicks could say anything, the quarter was flipping in the air, so Hicks called heads. The coin struck the pavement, rolled, and came up tails.

They broke if off in a style that Scott would have admired. "Anything I've got that'll catch a fish, you'll be welcome to it," Hicks promised.

"Same here," Moseley said.

Over on the low hill across the parking lot, Randy Blaukat was seeing his options slip away in the face of his partner's reputation. Gary Klein was 28, only 4 years older than Blaukat, but he was already on his way to becoming a bass fishing legend. Klein had started fishing professionally right out of high school in Oroville, California, north of Sacramento. He had joined the B.A.S.S. circuit in 1979, and was already one of its top ten money winners. He was tall, slender, and blond. He exuded a typically California brand of outdoor wholesomeness, and the fact that he was friendly and almost always cheerful disguised the intensity with which he fished. He was also Rick Clunn's best friend.

Klein, like Blaukat, had admired Clunn from afar before meeting him in 1979. "I got along real good with Ricky right from the start," he said. "I'm not a person who goes along with the crowd, and that's Ricky, too."

Now, well into their friendship, both had experienced premonitions that they would win tournaments. Both had followed inner voices to sometimes unlikely fishing spots, and found in those places fish that won tournaments for them. Out of fishing grew a broader commonality. The two men shared many ideas outside of bass fishing. Klein believed that if people heard him and Clunn driving down the road swapping thoughts about positive thinking, motivation, confidence, and life in general, they would think of the two, "They ain't bass fishermen."

Klein was steamrolling Blaukat in his friendly, aw-shucks, sunny California kind of way. "I've got two little areas, and we're gonna go for the gusto first thing, because that's when they're eating, first thing in the morning," he said. He told Blaukat he had caught 16 pounds by eleven o'clock on the first morning of practice, and the last bass he'd caught was followed by four others "just waiting to take the bait away." He said he was so confident of one spot, "I'm gonna bust a 20-pound string out of there, there ain't no doubt about it."

Blaukat agreed to ride in Klein's boat to Klein's fish. But he held on to his final prerogative, the right to stand shoulder to shoulder at the front of the boat instead of fishing "used" water from the back. "I want it understood," he said, "that I'm gonna be up front fishing with you."

Later Blaukat said assertively, "I'll give him his chance, and if it's not paying off we're going to my water."

The Chicamauga Marina occupies TVA land on the lakeshore above the southern end of Chicamauga Dam. The entrance road curves to the right around a protected cove that holds neat rows of tin-roofed boat sheds, turns to follow a generous cut joining the marina with the lake, and doubles back on itself at a wide boat-launching ramp that overlooks the lake and dam. Here, dim light gathering behind the yellow pines that stood around the cove, the fishermen assembled on the morning of June 4.

At six-thirty, responding to Dewey Kendrick's bullhorn, drivers began moving their boats out of the formless mass milling in the cut and into single-file procession for the morning checkout. As they idled past the floating dock where B.A.S.S. officials handed them flags and checked their safety gear and live wells, the fishermen wore faces that were grim and determined, nonchalant, or simply dazed with sleep.

Blaukat had spent a sleepless night. After he had spooled new line onto his reels, sharpened his hooks, organized his plastic worms by shape and color, and set his rods and tackle by the door of the room, there had been nothing left to do but worry. He longed for the night to be over and for the day to start. He kept repeating, "I am so nervous," as if saying the words would expel his uncertainty. To occupy himself still further, he inscribed words of inspiration on the bill of his white Ranger Boats cap. "Go for it! #1," he wrote.

Now, floating in the cut in Klein's boat, waiting for their call to move through the line, Blaukat was still nervous, but grateful that the waiting was almost over. "As soon as I get that first fish in the boat I'll be breathing easier," he said.

Moseley dealt with his nervousness by going out into the Chattanooga night. He said if he didn't go out, he would think about going out, and that would ultimately be more distracting than if he just went ahead. When Moseley picked up Hicks at twenty after six that morning, he had had as little sleep as Blaukat. He felt that this helped rather than hurt his fishing, for it reduced his reactions to instinctive levels. "I find that if I haven't had any sleep, I set the hook right away instead of thinking about it and playing around to make sure he's got it," he said. "It improves my fishing."

While Moseley waited, Hicks beside him, for their starting call, Roland Martin was moving through the line. As he did, the blond golden bear of bass fishing stuck a radio antenna into a mounting slot on his boat's gunwale long enough to call the lock tender. "Heading that way," he said. "Be there in about a minute." Then

he was gone in a cloud of spray to lock through to Nickajack.
There was suddenly the thought that Moseley had been right about
the lower lake.

But Moseley turned his boat upstream and began a ten-minute
run to Dallas Bay, the long, irregular inlet off the west side of the
river course where Hicks had found good fishing. Hicks had been
optimistic when he told Moseley they'd catch a limit in half an
hour. But each man had seven fish in his live well by eleven that
morning.

Both Moseley and Hicks began to cull as soon as they had limits.
The idea was to catch larger fish, and release their smaller keepers to build up a winning weight. In the afternoon, Moseley persuaded Hicks to fish Harrison Bay, on the opposite side of the
lake. He took them to the shallow bed of milfoil grass where he
had caught the two bass in two casts on Monday afternoon. Hicks
caught his two largest fish on Moseley's spot, but Moseley did not
improve his catch.

Harold Sharp and the B.A.S.S. tournament staff had comman-
deered for the weigh-in site a parking area at the edge of the cove
opposite the marina docks. The B.A.S.S. trailer, its side converted
to a scoreboard, blocked one end of the site. Low bleachers were
placed at the foot of a grassy berm rising to the road above. The
prize boats and vans were on display, and the Chattanooga Bass
Club sold food and drinks from small concession stands. A bargelike floating dock provided mooring space for the boats of the returning fishermen. They followed a catwalk to the shore and the
row of water troughs leading to the locus of the site, Ray Scott's
stage, the raised weighing stand.

At four o'clock, when the first boats arrived, the bleachers were
full and people wearing bright summer clothing sprawled on the
grass in the warm sun. A cadre of small boys, wearing the yellow-
and-white caps of B.A.S.S. volunteers, hovered at the foot of the
scales waiting for fish to be weighed so they could return them to
the water. Scott's drawl, booming over the loudspeakers, signaled
the beginning of the weigh-in.

Clunn brought in a limit of small keepers weighing 7 pounds
and 1 ounce. It was enough to assure him of his thirteenth visit to
the Classic. But Clunn aimed to win the tournament, and he had

not made even the top twenty. "I need to catch eleven or twelve pounds tomorrow to stay in the running," he said. Still, he saw no reason to change what he was doing. "The quality fish aren't there," he said. "So to go out and look for big fish would be a mistake. My plan for tomorrow is just to go out and get bit seven times."

Joe Thomas weighed-in two small keepers. "I was nervous this morning, but now I'm in miracle range," he said about his dwindling prospects for the Classic. Tauber was in better shape, but none too secure, with a nearly 6-pound catch. In the fight for Angler of the Year, Mickey Bruce lost ground and Brauer, Houston, and Nixon gained.

For Blaukat and Moseley, the tension they had felt that morning gathered and swelled, like a storm that refused to break, and by the weigh-in's end nothing had happened to relieve them.

Blaukat had outfished his better-known partner. Klein caught just one fish, and Blaukat three. But they were small, a total of 2 pounds and 6 ounces, and Blaukat remained in agony. He calculated that his pad—the weight by which he was above the bare minimum to make the Classic—was down to 3 pounds.

Moseley's fish weighed 7 pounds, 6 ounces, making his catch weight for the year 89 pounds and 7 ounces. He calculated that he had inched up toward the Classic, but he needed great strides. When the "7-6" flashed on the digital readout, Scott covered up the microphone with one hand and spoke quietly to Randy. "Next year's the year," he said.

"It's not over yet," Moseley replied. He said later he had lost a 3-pounder at the boat fifteen minutes before he and Hicks had stopped fishing. It would have given him a catch to almost match Hicks's 10 pounds, 13, and the prospect of a 10-pound day left him with a shred of hope remaining. He had no choice but to look for big fish. On Thursday, he vowed, he would go to Nickajack. "I'm going to gamble," he said. "I'm going to go down there for two hours, and if nothing happens, I'm coming right back."

By the time they sat down to dinner that night at Shoney's, Blaukat had developed a twitch in one eye, and he kept saying, "Tomorrow is the most important day of my life. I've got to catch a limit. I've just got to." He picked at a salad, and entreated Moseley for advice. "I've got to hit that riprap at the nuclear plant, don't I? Where's the best spot to fish at in those two bays with that Rapala? You definitely think the Rapala is the key, over the Rogue?"

Moseley gobbled spaghetti, chatted up the waitress, and reassured Blaukat, "The Classic can be had tomorrow, no problem, for both of us. You watch me tomorrow, Randy. I'm gonna have a huge string of fish. I am. Ten pounds."

Roland Martin's day on Nickajack had produced one fish. It weighed a pound.

An amazing grapevine operates among the fishermen. It is amazing because it seems to work on the water, when the fishermen are scattered hither and yon, so that by the time they return from the day's fishing everyone seems to have heard something about what everyone else has caught. It turns out that the grapevine is the result not of strange phenomena or telepathic skills but of the B.A.S.S. camera crews scuttling among the leading fishermen and passing on the latest catch reports. In any case, word reached the weigh-in that Jimmy Houston had had a big day and it looked like he had beaten out Brauer for Angler of the Year.

There were no predictions for the lower end of the order, where anxiety was running strong. Tauber was among the first in, and his four fish weighed 7 pounds and 14 ounces. "Rich is going to make it," Joe Thomas said, his weight lifter's body sagging in weary counterpoint to his bright ensemble of red logo shirt and white shorts, tennis shoes, and socks, as he approached the scales with a much lighter catch.

The scoreboard showed 3 pounds and 4 ounces, and Thomas told Ray Scott, "I think I'll go home and sleep awhile."

"You were in it right up to the end," Scott said.

"Yeah, but now I guess I'll have to watch the Classic on TV."

Thomas walked from the weighing stand into the crowd of fishermen that was gathering behind the B.A.S.S. bus. Already, a subtle segregation had begun. Tauber was animatedly describing his day's big fish to Gary Klein. "I fought him all over the place, got him to the boat, got my thumb in his mouth, and I locked down on him. And when I did, that chugger just fell out of his mouth. God was smiling down on me, and gave me one."

Klein had been fishing within view of Tauber. "I was pulling for you," he said. "I was happy when you got it in the boat." Klein was already assured of being in the Classic.

Thomas stood with his arms folded across his chest, absorbed in his own thoughts. Interrupted, he gave a rueful, tight-lipped smile and said, "It's tough. Three years in a row, it's getting kind of old. You've got to put on a face in front of everybody. But later, when you're driving home, you can let it show."

Blaukat weighed-in with four slender, bantamweight bass. He had fished all morning and into the afternoon before he caught the first at one o'clock. One had died, and with the 2-ounce penalty that cost him, his weight for the day was 3 pounds and 3 ounces. He moved to the side and began writing numbers—pounds and ounces—on a sheet of paper. "If I win it or lose it, it'll be by ounces," he said.

Houston's return to the weigh-in caused a stir. A camera crew climbed aboard his boat and stuck a camera lens practically into the live well as Houston removed his fish, then followed him to the stand. "Jiimmmy Hoouuuuston," proclaimed Ray Scott.

Cortney and Brooke met Clunn at the dock. He looked particularly intense, and his first words to Brooke were, "What's the big fish?" Then he started digging in his live well and placing bass after bass into his bag. One was a beauty, a slab-sided lunker that struggled violently when Clunn lifted it, and kept flapping after it was in the bag.

Somebody said, "Moseley scratched."

At that moment, Moseley's boat was gliding toward the dock. He dragged his right hand across his throat.

The B.A.S.S. computers eventually confirmed what the fishermen had already figured out by adding figures on their rumpled sheets of paper. Jimmy Houston won Angler of the Year. Randy Blaukat made the Classic by 1 pound. He placed thirty-third among the thirty-five qualifiers, 4 ounces behind Rich Tauber. Moseley's first-day partner, Tom Hicks, had made the field. Thomas and Moseley had fallen short.

Moseley placed a hand on Thomas's shoulder. "We'll be there next year, man," he said.

"I hope so," Thomas replied.

"There are a lot of upset puppies here," observed Thomas's girlfriend, Becky Wing of Cincinnati.

It was hard for Blaukat to be as happy as if Moseley had made the Classic, too. While Moseley busied himself congratulating others, Blaukat tried earnestly to share the credit with his friend. "He put me on that bait," he told anybody who would listen. "I threw that Rapala of his all day. I didn't even have one."

Tauber likewise included Thomas in his account of his successful day. He had lost a big fish, he said, and thought, "There goes the Classic. Then I remembered something Joe and I had talked about. It wasn't over. I could still catch a limit. I kept casting, and I caught another keeper, and then I caught a duplicate of the one I lost."

Moseley's defeat was doubly disappointing. He had not only failed to make the Classic. By failing to land even one keeper, he had finished 101st, 2 ounces short of the top 100, in the Super-Invitational, which would continue tomorrow. He was, he said, a victim of commerce on the river. He had gone to the lock for the passage to Nickajack, but a barge was going through. He made a pass along the face of the dam, and "lost a big one and two others." When the lock was cleared and refilled, he locked through with other fishermen, including Jimmy Houston. "And I decided to come back early and that was my mistake. They stayed down there. I fished in sight of them for an hour and a half. And I lost two, including a 2- or 3-pounder there." He had lost five fish altogether, he said, and caught at least eight fish too short to keep.

Blaukat returned to the Scottish Inn to find that three cards had arrived from his girlfriend, Shauna Mathis, back in Joplin. Shauna sent Blaukat off to each tournament with the gift of a single long-stemmed red rose. Her cards were printed with butterflies and flowers and verses that were equally expressive of the way she felt about him: "I keep thinking I couldn't love you more...and then keep finding that I do."

"Well, I gotta call the wife, I mean the girlfriend," Blaukat said. While Moseley stared blankly at a *Trapper John, M.D.* rerun, Blaukat spoke to Shauna. "Well, I made it," he said quietly, pride and relief mixing in his voice. "I just squeaked in." He smiled wearily, and later turned down an invitation to go out and celebrate. "I think I'm ready for bed," he said. "I don't think you realize the strain I just went through. I'm a noodle."

Moseley's call to Jean was one that she had dreaded. She heard him say, "Well, I didn't make the Classic, and I didn't make the cut." The resignation in his voice came through, and she wished that she could be there with him. The thought she sometimes had, that she couldn't take another year of waiting and hoping for a future that seemed always just out of reach, dissolved in that instant, and she was prepared to do whatever it took to help Randy to realize his dream. "I'm behind him all the way," she said later. "He deserves to win. He gives it his all. I'll be able to endure another year, or longer if that's what it takes."

Whatever doubts he might have felt inside, there was no more talk from Moseley about leaving the circuit. He said he was "relieved that the year's over, because now I've got next year to look forward to." He talked again about needing to line up financial sponsors.

Blaukat had also missed the top-100 cut, but had to stay for Classic photographs. Moseley, with nothing to keep him in Chattanooga and a guide trip scheduled back on Lake of the Ozarks, lingered as if he could not tear himself away from his vanished possibilities. He and Rick Johnson went along with Joe Thomas and Becky Wing for a desultory late meal, and Moseley watched television late into the night. The next morning he slowly and lackadaisically loaded his gear into the boat for the trip home. He untied his lures and returned them to their tackle boxes—the jigs in one, worms in another, top-water plugs and crankbaits in another. He replaced his rods and reels in the Ranger's rod locker. Finally, he locked the boat down on its trailer, and fitted and tied the blue tarpaulin. Blaukat could not remember seeing Moseley quite so down. When everything was ready, Moseley still could not face the road. He sank down in front of the television. George Hamilton was playing a weak-willed son struggling to impress his autocratic southern planter father, played by Robert Mitchum, in a hoary melodrama called *Home from the Hill*. Moseley watched it till the end, and then had no more excuses not to leave.

The tournament continued. Rick Clunn's 14-pound and 13-ounce catch the day before had moved him into second place in the Super-Invitational. That had earned him $4433 in the unusual split payout. Clunn saw in his standing an opportunity not only to win the tournament but also to overtake Roland Martin as the B.A.S.S. all-time leading money winner. He was not quite $35,000 behind, $257,000 to Martin's $292,000. First or second place would move Clunn ahead of his rival, who had missed the cut.

With a hundred fishermen left in the tournament, the first-place man was paired with the fifty-first, the second with the fifty-second, and so on. Clunn's partner was one-time Classic winner Tommy Martin of the so-called Hemphill gang. Martin, 45 years old, had an anachronistic set of sideburns swooping down his leathery cheeks, in contrast to the blow-dried hairstyles of the Moseleys and Taubers on the circuit.

"He's a good fisherman," said Clunn. "One of us is going to figure it out."

While Clunn fought to overtake Roland Martin, other rivalries also were being fought out. They were contested off the water, for exposure in an over-$2-billion marketplace of more than 20 million bass fishermen. The most intense of these was between the Outboard Marine Corporation (OMC), maker of Evinrude and Johnson outboards, and Mercury Marine, owned by the Brunswick Corporation. OMC had been an early sponsor of B.A.S.S. events, but Mercury had dominated the B.A.S.S. tournament circuit since OMC had withdrawn in 1979; by 1986, thirty-three of the top fifty Angler of the Year finishers ran Mercury or Mariner—the same engine with a different cowl—outboards. But OMC had returned aggressively to the tournament trail in 1985. The company outbid Mercury to be B.A.S.S.'s official outboard, which meant that Evinrude or Johnson outboards, not Mercuries, drove the identical boats fishermen used in highly visible contests like the Mega-Bucks finals and the Classic. Now, OMC was raiding Mercury's stable of fishermen.

Orlando Wilson was one of the first professional fishermen Mercury sponsored. Their relationship went back fifteen years or more. Wilson was still practically a boy, a voluble, entertaining cutup fishing local and regional tournaments, when Mercury began providing him an engine. As Wilson became more visible, and his television show moved from a local Atlanta station to national exposure on Ted Turner's WTBS, the company's stake in Wilson grew. By the first half of 1986, Mercury was paying Wilson $35,000 a year and providing engines for use on his show, in exchange for "promotional considerations." Those included mention in the credit roll at the end of the show. And Wilson always used a Mercury outboard.

But when OMC agreed to pay $200,000 to become a full spon-
sor of *Fishin' with Orlando Wilson,* starting in the fall of 1986, Wilson
started fishing with an Evinrude.

Landing such high-profile fishermen was of "ultimate impor-
tance" to Evinrude's marketing effort, said Larry Koger, the portly,
congenial manager of special markets for OMC's Evinrude product group. "We're looking for that guy running that aluminum
fishing boat with a six or eight horsepower, who's watching these
people on TV and seeing magazine articles about them. The buy-
ing public emulates people who are leaders in the field," he said.

Koger was always alert to new leaders emerging. Now, as the
Super-Invitational continued, he was snatching one from under
Mercury's nose. Zell Rowland, who lived on the other side of Montgomery, Texas, from Rick and Gerri Clunn in the condominiums
near Lake Conroe, was a young fisherman on track for the Classic. Rowland, 29 years old, rail-thin and painfully reticent, used a
Mercury that the company provided him at cost, and Koger thought
he had the bait to make Rowland switch: an engine for free if
Rowland made the Classic field. When Rowland cemented a Classic spot and moved into the Super-Invitational lead on the second
day, Koger reeled him in and Rowland, with the Mercury still on
his boat's stern, was suddenly faced with the unusual problem of
demonstrating his new loyalties. By the end, he was fishing in a
borrowed, Evinrude-powered boat and wearing an Evinrude cap
in all his interviews.

Koger demonstrated prescience, because Rowland went on to
win the Super-Invitational. Clunn slipped to third during his day
of fishing with Tommy Martin. On the fourth and final day, Saturday, June 7, he slipped further. Returning to the dock, he held
up six fingers and then held his hands apart to indicate the size of
the fish he was bringing in. His hands were not far apart. Clunn's
catch weighed 5 pounds and 3 ounces, landing him in sixth place
overall. Anyone but Clunn might not have been dissatisfied.

"I hate to work this hard and not do well, or not as well as I
wanted," he said, sitting on the edge of a water tub and signing
autographs after the weigh-in was complete. He had finished 5
pounds and 7 ounces behind Rowland, whose winning total was
39 pounds, 6 ounces. But late in the day, Clunn had lost a 3- to
5-pounder that could have moved him into second place. He had
done everything he could to save the fish, submerging his rod tip

to keep the bass from jumping and shaking the hook, but the bass was too quick for him.

"The next thing I knew he was gone. And that destroyed me mentally. I knew I needed that fish and one other fish to win, and it was just too late. I kept fishing hard, but my mind was somewhere else. If I had caught those two fish...I really wanted to take over as the all-time money winner."

Brooke and Cortney, wearing rainbow-colored playsuits, waited, fidgeting a little. Gary Klein walked over, and Cortney hugged him. "Hello, munchkin," he said. "Your dad didn't win. You didn't cross your fingers. You needed to cross your toes, too."

Clunn smiled. Cortney waited for a break in the autograph seekers, hugged her father, and asked, "Go swimmin'?" Small boys fished around the cove, where nearly 1900 bass had been released during the four-day tournament. The summer afternoon belonged to children at play. The fishermen would work again next month, when the U.S. Open took them to Lake Mead, in the Nevada desert, in the searing heat of mid-July.

# The U.S. Open

Rick Clunn thought that in another life he must have been a desert Indian. He was not sure he believed in reincarnation, but he was willing to consider the possibility. Especially lately, since reading Shirley MacLaine. The dry desert heat cleansed and purified him, reduced his work to an essence that was part instinct, part survival. The elements were magnified in the desert: the earth was more raw and harsh, the sky closer, all life more delicately balanced. Clunn felt he was part of that balance. The desert enfolded and absorbed him, bringing him close to the perfect intuition that he sought.

On August 26, 1983, Clunn had had a vision in the desert. Not precisely in the desert, but lying awake in his bed at the Tropicana Hotel in Las Vegas, wondering how he was going to come from thirteenth place, 6½ pounds out of first, on the last day of the U.S. Open on Lake Mead, where a 5-pound bass in August is as rare as a shade tree. "I've blown it," Clunn was thinking to himself. "I've got myself out of it. I'm six pounds behind. So I've got to go for some big fish." And as he lay there, his mind on tomorrow's fishing, a scene appeared to Clunn. "I got this real clear vision that I'm going to catch two five-pounders. Like I said, catching a five-pounder on Lake Mead in August is almost impossible."

On August 27, he ran 115 miles up the lake into the Colorado
River and the Grand Canyon, amid umber striations. Cliff Craft,
who was with Clunn that day, remembers that it was over 100°F,
and that he and Clunn covered their faces against the burning
wind. The water was higher than it had ever been, turning dry
gulches into shallow coves, and layered, like a parfait; the cold,
muddy Colorado River water lay below 3 feet of clear water, in
which the fish swam in full view. Clunn began fishing with a plastic worm in a cove, among live tamarisk trees that for the first time
were in the water. "And the first fish I caught was five, and the
last fish I caught was five."

That afternoon, Clunn weighed-in 14½ pounds, won the $50,000
tournament, and entered his era of mental exploration. "I finally
said, 'Wait a minute. There's something here that my mind is doing for me that I'm not allowing it to do most of the time.' And
that's when I really started delving in and trying to change this
thing from an unconscious happening to a conscious happening.
How can I consciously control this?"

He had been listening to the tape of *Jonathan Livingston Seagull*
for ten years by then. "I couldn't even tell you at that point that
Richard Bach was the one who wrote it," he said. "I just liked what
it said. I liked the concept of going from one level to the other,
you know, and striving for perfection and yet, really, there is no
such thing as perfection. That made sense to me. Everything in it
made sense to me. Setting no limits. No limitations. But I didn't
know where it came from. And yet I felt that somewhere in that
tape was the key, and I started listening to that tape, and I also
started looking for tapes and books on the mind.

"A lot of them were frustrating. You'd get them, and they were
psychocybernetics, which is a very mechanical way of controlling
the mind. And I got into reading those, and I understood what
they were saying, but they didn't really say where they came from,
why does this work, they only said this is the way to do it. That
still didn't really satisfy me."

It was not until he found U. S. Andersen's *The Magic in Your
Mind* on a trip to San Francisco that, for Clunn, "everything started
falling into place. First of all, it explained so much of what was
in *Jonathan Livingston Seagull*. It was pretty well parallel to it. I
didn't like a lot of it at first, because it dealt with a lot of religious
things."

Nonetheless, Clunn found in the Andersen book what he had been seeking, a methodology to "turn an unconscious effort to a conscious effort.

"The basic premise behind it is that we are all simply a thought of a supreme thought, and even though we're even [a small] part of that supreme thought, all the knowledge that is within the supreme thought is also within you, if you want to use it. All the answers to everything are within your mind already. You don't have to be taught from a book, you don't have to be educated about it, and the best way to show that this is true is the artistic minds, the Mozarts, the Michelangelos, the great scientists. Almost in every case, they'll tell you that their gift, or their art, came from someplace else. It didn't come from them. Like Mozart's music. He was a child prodigy. He was writing perfect music, without mistakes, that had never been written before. Did you watch the movie *Amadeus*, by any chance, where the guy looked at him and said, 'This did not come from this funny little man. These are the works of a supreme artist. This is actually the music of God,' implying that there's a higher thought process that is giving you that knowledge? It shows up in the artistic mind. That's why so many artists are, well, I don't know what would be the terminology, because they live in a society that is totally against the way their minds work, and that's why so many of them are...kind of outcasts, and not accepted, especially in their own times.

"Finally, after studying this for about a year and a half, I decided to actually go through this process that's in the book for trying to make this unconscious thing appear consciously for me. And I went through it, and the first time I tried it was the event at Okeechobee."

Preparing for the B.A.S.S. Florida Invitational tournament on Lake Okeechobee in May 1985, Clunn "started visualizing. The first step is basically based on your imagination. Anything you can imagine can come true, done correctly. It can't just be a dull thing. You've got to get a clear visualization, over and over until it becomes crystal clear. It can't be a foggy picture in your mind.

"So I started working on this, like three weeks before Okeechobee, just imagining I'm going to go down there, I'm going to catch seven fish a day, and I'm going to catch two big fish every day, and that'll be enough to win the tournament. Every day I'd spend a certain amount of time just mentally getting this image of what

I was going to do. I was visualizing myself working a spinnerbait in this grass catching fish. But it's funny. I'm visualizing a spinnerbait and all of a sudden as I'm going through this visualization, over and over, all of a sudden I'd get this image of myself pitching a worm, and I'd notice and say, 'Wait a minute. That ain't what I'm going to do.'

"So anyway, that's what they call the affirmation period, getting this very, very clear visualization. One of the final things is called the absorption period. And I didn't understand the absorption period for a long time. I may not understand it all, really, yet. But what the absorption period is, for me, it's getting on the water in practice and shutting out all distractions, all human distractions, even your own. If you listen to the boat-talk, or the dock-talk, about some guy that caught thirty pounds last night, and he's throwing this bait, those are all distractions. You get out there and you become part of the environment. Basically, you are the environment anyway. The knowledge of everything out there is within you. You've just got to allow it to start flowing through you. And so, basically I get out there and I work hard and I'm working so hard and getting so fatigued that I shut a lot of my normal senses down. In a lot of these books you'll read about these scientists, Louis Pasteur and these people, when they finally made their discoveries it came after years of fatigue. A lot of things came to them after they got depressed that they weren't going to find the answer. They almost just shut all their human faculties down, and all of a sudden the answer came to them. And that's what the absorption time does for me. When I get on the water—that's why practice is so critical—I've got to become part of the environment. I've got to see the minnows, and feel the way the water feels, and read the reeds and the way the wind is blowing and the way the current's moving, and you just become part of it. And that's when your intuitive mind starts giving you the answers.

"And what happened in that tournament is, the first day I went out and caught a limit of fish, and had two big fish, just like I'd imagined. The funny thing was, I found those fish with a spinnerbait in practice, just like I'd envisioned, and we'd had windy days in practice. The first day of the tournament it slicked off—dead calm, bright sun. And that's where my knowledge complemented my intuition. I knew that the spinnerbait was over. Immediately.

I didn't even pick the spinnerbait up the first day of the tournament. I picked up the flippin' stick and started pitching a worm, just like my thoughts kept changing me over.

"It wasn't all perfect, though. The next day I went out, caught my limit. Instead of catching two big fish, though, I caught three big fish. The third day, I went out, caught my limit, but I only caught one big fish. The numbers were still the same. I just didn't have the exact days right. But I had a limit every day and six big fish in the tournament.

"The only other thing about the tournament that I knew, I kept getting this vision, when I was thinking about it, that it was going to be a matter of ounces, which it turned out being, a matter of ounces. Even that last day, I'm sitting there thinking, 'I know I'm not doing as good as I was doing, but I'm still going to win. I'm just going to barely win it, but I'm still going to win it.' I kept getting this vision of barely winning it, by a few ounces."

The scene at the weigh-in that day was as dramatic as Clunn had imagined it. He weighed-in early, and Roland Martin came to the scales needing 19 pounds and 5 ounces to tie. Martin had a good catch. Ray Scott milked the tension, telling the crowd Martin could catch fish in a wet wagon track, as Clunn stood by uneasily. Martin's basket of fish went on the scales, and the digits on the display over Scott's head flashed "19-5." The crowd murmured, expecting a sudden-death fish-off. But Martin did a little turn away, and gave a disgusted little kick. One of his fish was dead, and Clunn's measure of victory was Martin's 2-ounce penalty.

"It was almost like something killed Roland's fish," Clunn continued. "Because Roland don't lose fish. Now, I'm not going to go that far. All I know is, there's a lot more up here"—he tapped the side of his head—"than most of us even begin to realize. And I'm not going to profess that I'm anywhere near mastering it. I'm just primitive in the sense of trying to touch what's really going on, what's all there and how we can use it."

Distractions, Clunn said, kept him from using the method to win every tournament he fished. "It takes time," he said. "It's hard to do because you're constantly fighting your own battles. The phone rings, a guy calls you up, your sponsor's pissed off about something, and your mind gets back in the real world where all

these distractions are. You know, your insurance guy says your
premiums are going up, so you get back in the material world.

"This is why so many of these people like Ralph Waldo Emerson and Walt Whitman, they were almost hermits. Even if they
were living in a big city, they lived in a little place and they kind
of stayed to themselves, you know. It wasn't because they disliked
people. It was because they could not be themselves with the distractions all around them."

The desert was Clunn's hermitage. It gave him greater access
to his recesses of thought. He found its starkness peaceable and
calming. The abrupt, unequivocal shear between survival and fail-
ure made things clear to him. It was clear to him now that he must
have an affinity with the desert, for not only had he won the U.S.
Open on Lake Mead in 1983, but the Red Man All-American in
which he had won $100,000 in the fall of 1985 had been held on
Lake Havasu, in Arizona. "The desert lakes have been good to
me," he said. That was when he said he thought he might have
been a desert Indian.

The 1986 U.S. Open was due to start in four days. It was Saturday, July 12, and the parking lot at the Tropicana Hotel and casino in Las Vegas was full of boats on trailers. The boats seemed
out of place. They bore no visible relationship to their surroundings. There was no water anywhere in sight, as far as the eye could
see, out to the mountainous rim of the stark valley in which the
neon and concrete city squatted. Within the landscaped, block-
square Tropicana compound, mechanical dinosaurs had been installed. They were situated near the pool, where they surveyed
the lustrous brown bodies with carnivorous intent, and they looked
slightly more at home than the boats outside. Now and then, one
of the dinosaurs would move arthritically, and utter a grievous
tape-recorded howl, but they were difficult to hear over the salsa
band and all the waterfalls.

Through this prehistoric evocation marched a diminutive Japanese fisherman in shorts, carrying a tackle box and a handful of
rods. The hooks on his lures were covered in neat plastic sheaths.
He walked down a hall and through the casino and disappeared
into an elevator, attracting no attention whatsoever.

July is a hot month in the desert. All Las Vegas vibrates with the thrum of giant compressors pumping cold air into the casinos. Outside, the dry air quivers with the heat, and wrings moisture out of plants and animals. The U.S. Open is as much endurance contest as fishing tournament. It is the only bass tournament where fishermen are allowed out of their boats; they can dive into the water to save themselves from heat stroke. First held in 1981, the Open was the first tournament that paid the winner $50,000, and is generally credited with pushing rival Ray Scott and B.A.S.S. toward bigger purses. U.S. BASS, the sponsoring organization, had some rocky times in 1985. Prize checks had been bouncing. Originally Western Bass, U.S. BASS had been taken over near the end of the year by two former tournament fishermen, Don Doty and Rick Seaman. As the Open approached, stability seemed to be returning.

U.S. BASS operated a draw tournament circuit much like the B.A.S.S. invitationals, with a world championship among top qualifiers. Those tournaments did not have the weight of the B.A.S.S. events, but the U.S. Open ranked with the BASS Masters Classic in its potential to establish a fisherman's career. Rich Tauber had won the Open in 1982, when he was 24. The success that followed put Tauber on an ever-growing schedule of appearances. He left his Woodland Hills, California, home for the Indianapolis Boat Show on the day after Christmas 1985, and it was June before he was home for more than a few days at a time. During one twenty-three-day stretch in February and March of 1986, he was in nineteen cities. "And that," said Tauber, "is obscene."

Western fishermen dominated the Open's entry list. Almost half the entries, and all the previous winners except Clunn, came from California and Arizona, and most had never fished the primarily Southern and Eastern tournaments of B.A.S.S. But the $50,000 winner's prize—all money, no boats or cars—lured many B.A.S.S. competitors into the desert. There was, as well, the lure of the casinos, for anyone who made his living at the unpredictable business of catching game fish was, in one way or another, a bettor through and through.

"You can't gamble without confidence," said Rick Clunn. "You can't fish for money without confidence."

Randy Moseley had arrived in Las Vegas on Friday. He had persuaded a handful of backers to stake his entry in the Open and had driven for three days from Missouri. He had reached the intersection of Fremont and the Strip when his van trembled and expired. At the hotel, his reservation had somehow gone awry. That night, he won $3500 rolling craps and playing blackjack, and lost it all back at the blackjack tables. On Saturday, he revived the van, spending $200 he could not afford having its starter replaced. That evening, when Jean arrived on a flight from St. Louis for what was to be a vacation, Randy felt obliged to tell her they were living one day at a time, as he had paid cash for the room and neglected to get a receipt. There was nowhere else to stay, since the tournament required fishermen to stay at the Tropicana. But they had a room for tonight, compliments of last night's high rolling, and tomorrow would take care of itself. That night at supper at a Mexican restaurant, Jean and Randy were cheerful and relaxed. She talked about her work at the Salt Box antique shop, and they described the house they hoped to build on the shore of Lake of the Ozarks.

On Sunday, July 13, Clunn rose quietly without disturbing Gerri, or Brooke and Cortney in the other bed. When he left for Lake Mead it was four-thirty in the morning. The road rose until, over his shoulder, twinkling Las Vegas looked like a wash of phosphorescence on the desert floor. Ahead, the mountains still were dark. Forty minutes from Las Vegas, the lake appeared over a rise, the pale light of day just beginning to reflect upon its surface. An oasis of green marked the Lake Mead Marina.

You could not see it from the rise, or even from the air, because the lake stretches 110 miles from end to end, but on a map Lake Mead appears vaguely like a ship's anchor, with the long, northward-pointing Overton Arm the shank and two broad, open basins, Gregg to the east and Boulder to the west, the flukes, linked by narrow canyons. The Colorado River flows east to west from fluke to fluke, the Virgin River descends from the north down the Overton Arm, and a third basin, the Virgin, opens at the conflux. Hoover Dam, the monumental drain plug that 5000 men worked day and night from 1931 to 1935 to build, stops up the outflow from the Boulder Basin at a point in Black Canyon, which exits to the south. The Lake Mead Marina is 5 miles northwest of the dam as the crow flies, and the lake's westernmost point, Las Vegas Wash, is another 8 miles in the same direction. Fifteen miles

due west from Vegas Wash will land you back at the gaming tables of Las Vegas.

Clunn began his day's work, as usual, with a definite plan. He
said the western reaches of the lake were "known for quality, but
also for inconsistency." That meant that big fish were caught there,
but not often. "But that comes from the locals," Clunn said. "They
fish mostly on weekends." He theorized that the anglers were so
busy trying to dodge roving bands of fun seekers on water skis
and jet skis that they might have overlooked consistent patterns.
"I thought I'd come down and try to develop some consistency,"
he said.

He took his first bass at six-thirty that morning, within sight of
the marina, on a bulge in the shoreline called Saddle Island for
its shape and the stirrup of land that kept it from being a true
island. It was a "situation fish," he said, that would have moved to
deeper, cooler water as the sun rose. Alternating between a spinnerbait and a minnow-shaped, shallow-running crankbait called a
"Long A," he worked around the Saddle Island shoreline, stopping only long enough to replace his trolling motor, when it suddenly broke down, with a spare he carried in the rod box of his
boat. A stiff wind blew from offshore, piling up a chop that slammed
the boat around, and Clunn scrambled to keep his footing on the
foredeck as he fished.

Sunrise illuminated the dark slopes of the Black Mountains with
a Georgia O'Keefe palette of earth colors, browns, grays, dun, and
dusty rose. Long shadows fell from peaks and ridges like knife
blades across the mountainsides.

North of Saddle Island, the rugged landscape gave the lake a
hundred coves. Clunn worked from one to the next, casting around
the drowned tamarisk, or salt cedar, shrubs that occupied the water close to shore. At seven forty-five, he aimed a cast into a weed
patch no bigger around than a large skillet and reeled a fighting
3½-pounder to the boat.

As the sun climbed higher, washing out the shadows, the mountains lost their sharpness and all their jagged edges melted in the
glare. The sun bore down from a cloudless sky. In the coves, camp-
ers began to stir. The angry buzz of jet skis faded in and out, and
skiers slashed the water. No tournament boats were anywhere in
sight.

A little after nine o'clock, Clunn had a spectacular run of fishing that lasted no more than thirty minutes. First, in a cove that ended in a small "V" leading to a clump of cattails, he had two quick strikes, one on the Long A and the other on a top-water plug. He hooked neither fish, but said they were nearly 2 pounds each. Using the different baits was part of his practice plan. "I'm trying to find a bait that hooks the fish that strike it," he said. "There are fewer fish down here, so it's important to convert your strikes. I've already had eight pounds of strikes."

Clunn switched to a spinnerbait and moved around a rock point to a wide cove backed with a rock levee. One side of the cove mouth, near a makeshift campground where a Volkswagen bus huddled in the shade of an awning, was shallow and scattered with salt cedars, both under the water and exposed. Making long casts among the shrubs, he caught two more keepers, the largest 2½ pounds, on successive casts. After he boated and released the second, he used a pair of needlenose pliers to bend the hook closed on the spinnerbait. He cast again, and felt another strike. In each of the next two coves bass hit his bait and followed it to the boat as he reeled in.

Clunn moved along the lake's western shore from cove to cove and ran to the terminus of Vegas Wash to fish some more, as the temperature climbed past 105°F. He soaked a hand towel in the water and placed it inside his cap so that it covered the back of his neck, and sipped frequently from a plastic jug of water. Blue-black ravens rose from the tamarisks' thin shade at his approach. Sunbathers lounged in beach chairs at the water's edge as their car radios blasted at high volume. Clouds formed, so small they looked like white marbles rolling in a blue plate sky. Entire posses of jet skis screamed about in close formation. The sun peaked and tilted down, and as the shadows returned, dust trails followed the weekenders driving away from the lake. Clunn fished doggedly until late afternoon. After his big run at midmorning, he caught just one other fish, a slender bass that was barely the Nevada keeper length of 13 inches. But on his second day of practice, he was beginning to think he had found the consistency he sought.

"If I can get five strikes a day, I can win down here," he said.

Moseley had lost the first day of practice to his van's malfunctioning starter. Much of the second was lost to sleep after he argued

late into the night with the hotel about his room; the afternoon
was left when he got onto the water, and he drove around scout-
ing likely locations while Jean took the sun. On the morning of
the third and final practice day, Monday, July 14, the alarm clock
rang and there were no distractions. Randy and Jean left before
dawn and drove 77 miles to a point on the lake near the Gregg
Basin. They wound through the Black Mountains and over Hoover
Dam into Arizona, and finally turned up the Detrital Valley toward their destination at Temple Bar. Flash flood warning signs
stood along low points in the road.

"It would be a lot quicker to come by boat, but three times as
expensive," Randy said.

Temple Bar is one of half-a-dozen sites around Lake Mead that
have been developed with marinas, campsites, restaurants, and the
like as part of the Lake Mead National Recreational Area. These
sanctuaries—the Lake Mead Marina at Boulder Beach is another—
are patches of green order on the rock-girt shoreline; date palms
line neat rows of trailer campsites, grass grows, the descent to the
water is paved smooth, and boats rest in slips at sturdy plank docks.

One of these places is as attractive as another in the rubble-
strewn desolation of the desert, but distant Temple Bar seemed
oddly popular. Clunn had not seen one competitor at the Lake
Mead Marina. When the Moseleys arrived at Temple Bar, half-
a-dozen tournament anglers were launching boats. This was where
the fishermen had come to find consistency. Sad-faced Charlie
Campbell, runner-up in the B.A.S.S. Super-Invitational the month
before, was among them. Randy greeted his fellow Missourian and
turned to replacing the line on all his reels.

As he worked, Jean sat on the dock and held the boat close
with her feet. Even in the early morning, heat blossomed behind
a layer of thin clouds. A fly buzzed, and Jean swiped at it. "That's
why I married her," Randy joked. "Don't have to buy a flyswatter."

"Yeah, and I married you for your money," she retorted, toss-
ing her brown hair.

Fish swam lazily under the dock in water so clear you could
see a penny on the bottom 6 feet down. The fishermen called it
"gin-clear," and used line as light as 6-pound test to counteract
the increased visibility. Schools of silver minnows flashed across
the bottom. The larger fish were striped bass, anathema to the

tournament fishermen because they weren't eligible in the competition but often struck the same lures the largemouths did. In order to catch largemouths, you had to keep the stripers off the hook. Moseley aimed a few casts down the length of the dock, and then headed east upstream.

From Temple Bar upstream, Lake Mead pinches into Virgin Canyon and opens out again in the Gregg Basin. Another canyon, Iceberg, follows, and then, except for a few open spots like Grand Wash Bay, God's Pocket, and Pierce Bay, the lake narrows progressively as it winds toward its origins in the Grand Canyon and the Colorado River. At the lower end of the lake, where Clunn was fishing, the distances seemed manageable, but here perceptions skewed. The surrounding mountains gave a perspective against which to view the size of things, and the landscape was so big it diminished everything that entered it. The lake's surface seemed to fall away downhill between the canyon walls.

Randy stopped first on the north shore of the lake, just before entering Virgin Canyon, and fished among some inundated conifers. Another tournament boat worked the same embankment, farther east. The clouds remained, and sent down light, occasional sprays of rain. Randy fished with a buzz bait, named for the turbine-like blades that cut the surface like a torpedo thrashing through the water, a cigar-shaped top-water bait called a Zara "Spook," and a spinnerbait. The cloud cover dictated his choice of lures.

He moved gradually upstream, exploring a sheltered pocket where the water was so clear and deep you could see huge pieces of timber tumbled like matchsticks on the bottom. He set himself for two strikes, but the fish eluded the hook. Gray bleached driftwood littered the shoreline 20 feet above the water from a time when the lake was much higher. The rocks were bleached, too, so that the entire shore was banded, like a freighter's waterline. In the Virgin, and then the Iceberg, canyons, rising arches of gray and tan and rose seemed hewn by a rough cathedral builder. Eroded strata hung like tenement laundry on the faces of the cliffs.

A flock of bighorn sheep watched from above as Randy cast the spinnerbait and buzz bait among a field of flooded salt cedars in a cove, and Jean talked about her family. She said her mother and grandmother, whose husband had been a criminal court judge, thought she should have married a lawyer. "They like Randy," she said, "but it's the profession. They think it's all play, you know? You're in a boat, out on the water....

"They worry about me, and that's fine. They want to be sure I'm doing the right thing. I was raised comfortably. We never had to scratch, or wonder where the money was coming from. But it's all money with them, and all I want is to be able to give Justin what I had: little things, a vacation once a year, that sort of thing."

The fishing was not going well. Late in the morning, Randy announced he wanted to return to the Temple Basin near the launch site, where he had caught fish previously. In the Iceberg Canyon, pockets of cold air alternated with 100°F dry heat. Two small airplanes carrying sightseers followed the canyon downstream, tilting on the air currents, and disappeared around a bend.

In the open Temple Basin, with the sun out now, Randy began fishing a plastic worm along a rock point, and switched to a crankbait to work the shore of an island in the middle of a bay. He spotted Charlie Campbell, alone in his boat, and another angler, fishing the low shoreline across the bay. "There must be something around here," he said. But the day brought no more strikes, and at about two-thirty in the afternoon he lifted the trolling motor and headed back to Temple Bar.

"Normally I'd keep on fishing," Randy said. But he had more talking to do with the hotel about the room, and he needed to make a phone call back home to Missouri, where it was two hours later, to see if the tackle shop that had helped stake his trip would send him some more money. Randy returned from the phone shaking his head. The store had been robbed the night before, the owner had said, but he would see what he could do.

At midafternoon, the desert heat was daunting. Some hoses had been switched in Moseley's van when he had had the engine rebuilt recently in Missouri, and the air conditioner blew onto the inside of the windshield. Jean felt that it was going to be a long week.

The final day of practice was followed by an off day. That was a concession to both the anglers and the Tropicana, for it meant the anglers could spend Monday night in the casino without the nagging thought of daybreak and nine hours of fishing in the boiling sun to distract them.

The long, low-ceilinged room was ajangle with the sound of slot machines and the rattle of chips. To one side, two steps up, was a room where men in tuxedos and women in evening gowns played the mysterious game of baccarat. The fishermen kept to the crowded main room, favoring the blackjack tables or a spot at someone's elbow where they could kibitz. Roland Martin, a gold Rolex watch on one wrist and a heavy gold bracelet on the other, played as a small crowd of fishermen watched; Moseley had over-heard Martin opening a $25,000 line of credit the night before.

Gerri Clunn, with her blond hair and high cheekbones, was a fixture at the $2 blackjack table. She and Rick sometimes came to Nevada gambling spots for New Year's Eve, when Rick enjoyed betting on the college bowl games. Rick moved restlessly from one table to another. He spent several minutes at a $5 table, sat in at a $25 table for a while, and then got up and moved again. When he settled down at a $5 table, he piled up $1500 in winnings during a hot streak in which he bet $50 and $100 on almost every hand.

Over among the slot machines, a young, light-haired Arkansas schoolteacher and fisherman named Keith Brashers watched as fellow angler Evalyn Duncan—U.S. BASS, unlike B.A.S.S., did not bar women from its tournaments—won two $1000 jackpots. "Gosh, she's lucky," Brashers thought to himself. "I hope I draw her for a partner."

Moseley was playing blackjack at a $5 table. Like Clunn, he gambled easily and decisively, without counting his chips before betting. He played as if money was no factor in the game. Jean watched him lose $200, and felt her stomach tightening into knots. He won $500, and she tried to make him leave the table. He paid no attention when she tugged at him, and after a while she left the casino and went to bed.

"I can't stand to see him lose," she said. "It makes me so mad. It makes me sick." She was so sick she thought she might be pregnant again.

At the table with Moseley for a time was a tall, black fisherman from Las Vegas named Carl Harris, who was wearing a straw cowboy hat, jeans, and a jacket with no shirt. Moseley saw Harris the next day, and told him he'd stayed in the casino until seven in the morning, winning and losing $3200.

"Boy, you crazy," Harris said.

But his night at the tables got Moseley's room comped again. He nonetheless continued to insist loudly to anyone who would listen that his predicament was all a forgetful desk clerk's embarrassing mistake.

U.S. BASS had hired Jimmy Houston, the giggling fisherman fresh from winning Angler of the Year honors with B.A.S.S., as its master of ceremonies for the Open. Houston, like Roland Martin, was a fishing millionaire who counted endorsements, a television show, instructional videos, and various products—Houston and Martin had competing sunglass lines, for example—among his sources of income. His giggle was in fact a high-pitched whinny, and his humor was direct and heavy-handed.

One of the Open's features was a series of seminars by top fishermen. Clunn's Tuesday presentation on top-water fishing was preceded by Houston's introduction. "He's got forty-five minutes," Houston said. "When I get through introducing him he'll have ten minutes. He'll be able to tell you everything he knows."

Clunn, cradling a rod in the crook of his elbow, said, "Why is it that every time Jimmy Houston introduces me, I feel like Rodney Dangerfield?"

Clunn had been "a pretty shy boy" in high school, his father had said, and the boy that Holmes Clunn remembered was still a nervous speaker if a practiced one. His energy flowed into his fishing rod: he wound the reel, he spun the rod like a baton, he pulled the rod tip down and let it spring. When he managed to leave the rod alone, he still used his hands to gesture and shape and illustrate his comments.

His talk was a mixture of the topic assigned and a wide-ranging assortment of homilies and information. He said his favorite top-water bait was an out-of-date chugger called a "Pop-R," by Rebel. The Pop-R had a white fox–hair tail and was reintroduced after he and other pros created a new demand. "I work it fast," he said. "Worked slow, any other chugger is just as good." He spun a yarn about bass swarming after "the ugliest buzz baits you ever saw," losing one of the two he had, and then hanging the survivor out of reach in a treetop with a spot in the Classic on the line. He assured his audience that when friendly rivals like he and Gary

Klein got together, "we compare notes but we don't tell each other where we fish." Surprisingly, he announced that he was getting strikes before eleven in the morning in coves in 1 to 5 feet of water.

"I cringed when you said that," Klein told him later. But Klein had practiced far away in the Virgin Basin, and had heard only vague reports about Clunn's practice. The reports said that "Ricky's close, but he's fishing the wrong side of things," Klein said. Most fishermen felt the fish were "in deep water, up against the banks."

The raised dais on which Clunn stood was at one side of the Tropicana's South Pacific Ballroom, a cavernous space carpeted with a florid combination of green, red, pink, and mauve. Folding chairs filled the center of the room facing the dais, and the sponsor-provided prizes for each day's big fish winner, Skeeter boats powered with 175-horsepower Mercury outboards, were parked around the edges. Unlike B.A.S.S., U.S. BASS set no horsepower limits on its outboard-powered boats. U.S. BASS staff members, tidily dressed in bright red shirts, scurried here and there under the gaze's of the Open's previous five winners, whose oversize photographs were displayed on the wall behind the dais.

Two more presentations followed Clunn's, and then the crowd in the room swelled for the four o'clock draw for the first day's partner pairings. The fishermen included Evalyn Duncan and another woman angler, Dee Everhart of Arizona. Duncan, a Houston, Texas, medical secretary and the wife of a dermatologist, was a vivacious 47, short, tanned, with attractively graying hair. She was a regular on the Bass'n Gal circuit, a pro tour for women, and fished many U.S. BASS events. She scoffed at the B.A.S.S. rule against women anglers.

"It's utterly ridiculous," she said. "Sex would be the last thing you'd think about. You're just so utterly concentrated. There can be a lot of money involved. You're inflamed with passion, all right… for bass fishing."

The field of fishermen also included a group of eleven Japanese men. They were sponsored by Dallas- and Tokyo-based trade consultant Aki Sawahata. Aki and an inexhaustible camera crew of two were videotaping the tournament activities, for he planned to eventually release fishing videos in Japan, where he said bass fishing was growing popular. A tournament circuit already existed, and among the Japanese contingent were several tournament winners and Masahiro Hiramoto, whose résumé in the Open program described him as the "leading Bass Man in Japan." His counterpart, Roland Martin, had received a hero's welcome on a Japanese tour earlier in the year. Aki explained that on Japan's smaller lakes the style of fishing was much different; boats, for example, were for the most part small aluminum craft powered by motors in the 40-horsepower range, rather than the high-powered fiberglass speedsters American fishermen favored. Aki himself represented Ranger Boats in Japan, and so far had sold one.

Houston gained the dais in a flying leap that sent his mop of sun-bleached hair bouncing off his forehead, and was joined on stage by Don Doty, the president of U.S. BASS. Doty, who had dark hair and strode about the premises as if always on some urgent mission, was compactly built and fastidiously groomed. Like his B.A.S.S. rival Ray Scott, Doty had a salesman's personality and line of patter, but with Houston, Doty—like Scott—was the straight man. Pacing back and forth trailing his microphone wire, he ran through a list of tournament rules and safety requirements that were substantially the same as those for B.A.S.S. The penalty for late check-in would be half a pound per minute, with all credit lost after fifteen minutes. Fishermen late for the draws would lose a pound from their next day's catch. Anglers without boats, including the Japanese fishermen, had the right to dictate the fishing half the time, and Doty himself would arbitrate disputes between drivers and riders.

"Oh, by the way," Doty said. "The prizes will be in cash. Green cash." The fishermen, remembering the bounced checks of the recent past, applauded.

The Japanese fishermen came to the stage wearing neckties and blue blazers, and Houston proceeded to butcher their names. "You probably think I have a funny name too, don't you?" he said as he stumbled and giggled. Aki translated, and the anglers shifted on their feet and smiled.

As the draw started, Houston said, "OK, any of you who get paired with these Japanese fishermen, you've got to watch these guys. If you're not careful, they're liable to dive in your live well and eat your fish for lunch."

The Japanese laughed politely at Houston's sushi joke, once Aki had explained what he had said.

Befitting the surroundings, the draw was done lottery-style, by spinning a drum containing cards with the names of the fishermen, and drawing out two cards at a time. Thus fishermen from the same town could be paired, another departure from B.A.S.S. rules, and whistles and catcalls greeted the pairing of two Las Vegas fishermen.

Keith Brashers, to his pleasant surprise, drew Evalyn Duncan as a partner. Gary Klein was paired with Daryle Lamonica, the former Oakland Raiders quarterback, now an insurance agent, who was trying out a new sports career as a bass fishing pro. "He'll stay in the back of the boat," Houston said. "He's used to staying back behind those centers." Clunn drew another Texan, San Antonio contractor Mike Kotara. Moseley's partner was Jeff Munson, who had won the Open in 1984. Moseley was happy at the pairing, and readily agreed to ride with the fisherman from Chico, California.

Odds published in the program established Rich Tauber as the favorite to win his second U.S. Open. Klein was the third favorite, at 9 to 2 odds, and Roland Martin came in next at 8 to 1. Clunn was not listed among the favorites, and the opinion persisted among the fishermen that Clunn, as someone had said to Gary Klein, was "fishing the wrong side of things."

"We'll know today, won't we?" Clunn said to Klein the next morning as they were making final preparations. He gave his friend a wink.

The morning of July 16 brought a restive wind across the desert. Red small-craft warning flags fluttered from flagpoles at the Calville Bay Marina, site of the tournament starts and weigh-ins, as pink light, dusted with clouds, rose behind the far mountains.

Calville Bay is an indentation in the northern shore of Boulder Basin. The marina is snugged into an east-facing back corner of the bay, so that as you stand at the marina looking out, the rising sun emerges from behind craggy low outcroppings on the left of the harbor entrance and silhouettes objects on the water against a field of fluid gold. By land, the marina is about forty-five minutes from Las Vegas. The fishermen approached it on a two-lane road that wound out of the desert and descended into the protected crescent of the bay. They launched their boats on either side of a staging dock that was separate from the main docks and boat slips of the marina, and convened at the staging dock to meet their partners.

One hundred thirteen boats floated in the inlet with their motors idling, sending up white smoke, when Doty waved his arms and every driver pulled his kill switch. A sudden silence filled the marina basin while wisps of exhaust smoke rose and disappeared. Then the Statler Brothers' recording of "The Star-Spangled Banner" filled the air, and the fishermen stood in their boats and held their visored caps over their breasts. At six o'clock, Rich Tauber in the first boat steered down the outermost dock of the marina. Officials looked into his live well, and handed him a number that would be checked that afternoon against his safe return. Then he turned right, toward the rising sun.

The water was deceptively calm in the protected inlet. The boats idled in a line toward the buoys marking the end of the no-wake zone. Then, as they accelerated to top speed, everyone turned across the sunrise and headed up the lake, their roostertail wakes in one procession. Clunn was in the second flight of boats to leave. His was the one boat that turned right and headed south.

As he and Kotara crossed Boulder Basin toward Saddle Island, Clunn was surprised to find the water relatively flat. Twenty- to thirty-mile-per-hour winds had been predicted, but they had not yet reached Clunn's fishing grounds. His mind began a series of calculations; if it stayed calm against all predictions, and against his experience in practice, the bait fish would move from the shore to deeper water and the bass would follow them: exactly what the other fishermen had predicted. Clunn's fish were top-water fish. A calm day would bring his performance down and improve the others'. But that was a loser's thought, what Clunn called negative programming, and Clunn erased it. He concentrated on adjusting his performance in order to win. It was early, and still cool. Before the sun rose and warmed the water, the bass were likely to be lying close to shore, and as long as the winds were light, Clunn could throw a light top-water plug with maximum efficiency. He chose the Pop-R, and with the sun over his left shoulder, began casting among the drowned salt cedars in the inlet to the south of Saddle Island. Half an hour later, he caught his first bass of the day.

Kotara, fishing from the stern casting deck and using a spinner-bait, caught two bass at almost the same time, one after the other. Clunn noticed Kotara's catches, in part because it was his duty to net his partner's fish, but he resisted the temptation to covet them. Clunn's second bass came an hour later, again on the Pop-R.

The sun broke across the mountains and the day grew hotter. Commuters were just going to work, driving into Las Vegas from the east along the Boulder Highway, and for them the day was new. Their workdays would begin when they reached the low towers of the city, but Clunn's already had begun, and it was time to adjust to a change in his environment. Because Clunn had noticed that the wind was rising. He switched immediately to a spinner-bait.

The heavier spinnerbait was easier to cast with accuracy in the wind. And the continuous retrieve that it required eliminated the momentary slackness in the line that made fishermen miss strikes with the jerky retrieve of top-water plugs like the Pop-R.

As the wind rose toward the predicted 20 to 30 miles per hour, Kotara caught two more fish. By eleven-thirty, Clunn also had two more.

The coves above and below Saddle Island all had pockets of the wiry salt cedars, and the thicker they were the more likely it was that bass would hold among them. The spinnerbait was relatively hard to foul—the hook turned inward between its two arms—and thus good for casting around the bushes. But the tough limbs sawed and weakened the cofilament line. A fisherman had the choice of retying his lure frequently to eliminate the damaged length, in which case he would lose time and fail to cover territory; or he could take the chance that his line would fail under the strain of a big strike. Clunn left little to chance, but he felt it more important to cover each foot of water. "You can't catch fish if the bait isn't in the water," he said. Just before noon, a bass hit the spinnerbait close to the boat. Clunn leaned back to set the hook, and the line parted with a flaccid "snap." He thought later the fish would have added 8 to 10 ounces to his weight.

The sun, high up now, was relieved only slightly by the hot wind. In Las Vegas, the high temperature was reported as 113°F. Neither Clunn nor Kotara caught a fish between noon and one-thirty. Clunn drank water and fruit juice, but he did not stop to eat. Their conversation was utilitarian. Clunn told Kotara when he wanted to move to a new spot, and Kotara would stop fishing and climb down from the rear casting deck into the passenger seat. Each, when he had hooked a fish, would ask the other to get the net.

At around one-thirty, making another pass through the area where the fish had broken his line, Clunn caught his fifth bass of the day. Almost immediately, Kotara caught his fifth.

They continued fishing, trying to improve their catch weights by culling smaller fish. At two-thirty, fifty minutes before he and Kotara were due to check in, Clunn caught a 2-pounder and returned a 1¼-pounder to the lake.

After the first day's weigh-in, Kotara led the tournament with 10.06 pounds on the fractional scale used by U.S. BASS. Clunn was in fourth, with 8.89.

Hirokazu Kawabe, 27, from Kanagawa-Ken, Japan, had been paired for the first day's fishing with Harold Allen, 41, from Batesville, Mississippi. Allen, a perennial Classic qualifier, enjoyed his whiskey and between that and the sun had a great bursting beano of a red nose that lay over to one side. His pronounced Quasimodo limp, the result of a hip defect he'd never bothered to have repaired, helped make him look dangerous and a little scary, though in fact he was neither. When they met after the draw to discuss the first day's fishing, Aki stood by as an interpreter. Allen announced immediately that he would not be able to remember "Hirokazu," and thus would call his partner "Hiro." The abbreviation appealed to Allen as both a nickname and a compliment, and it came out that way as Allen said it: Hero.

Aki interpreted, and Hero nodded, smiling.

"Even the best fishermen are struggling," Allen said. "We'll go to where I think I've got some fish, deep ones, and if they don't show up for the show we'll try something else, maybe some top water. That OK with you, Hero?" Hero nodded.

The next morning Kawabe appeared on the dock carrying his rods neatly strapped together, with the plastic guards all the Japanese fishermen used covering the treble hooks on his lures. Allen was wearing a white jumpsuit covered with sponsor logos. His face lit up when he saw his partner, and he helped him aboard with his rods and gear. After Hero was settled, Allen leaned toward him and spoke like a cowboy addressing an Indian in the old westerns. "You...ready to go...out there?" He waved an arm in the direction of the lake.

"OK," said Hero.

Allen's reputation as a pedal-to-the-metal boat driver was well known in American bass fishing. He drove at times with a gallant recklessness that a timid person would mistake for a serious death wish, as if he was Captain Ahab and the black bass was the white whale. None of this was known to his partner.

The morning's ceremony was calm enough: the dramatic silence when the engines all were killed at once, the strains of the national anthem across the water, the dignified procession past the dock and out into the lake. But when the prow of Allen's Skeeter crossed the no-wake buoys, he slammed the throttle forward and Hero's head snapped back. The boat leaped up as if alive and then flattened into a 60-mile-per-hour run. The waves, which had seemed small and gentle and inviting in the protected cove of Calville Bay, were quite different in the open reaches of the lake. Allen wrenched the wheel to the left, and the boat skidded in a wide turn and crossed the rising sun to Hero's right. Allen bent down behind the cowl with his hat turned backward, the wind tearing at his grizzled beard. Hero looked for something to grab onto to keep himself in the boat, and found a railing on his left. He thought his eyelids might turn inside out.

They entered the dim light of Boulder Canyon, and the canyon walls embraced the boat in arms of ochre and umber, black and gray and tan and rust, rising tortured strata hacked layer from layer by time and wind and water. They emerged from the canyon into the Virgin Basin, the widest stretch of water in Lake Mead. Here the wind was pushing up whitecaps. Allen's boat slammed and skipped over the waves, throwing up clouds of spray. In Japan, rough water was a cause for slowing down, but to Hero's horror Allen showed no sign of reducing the boat's careening speed. Hero could not keep himself attached to the seat. He renewed his desperate grip on the gunwale rail. The waves piled up under the starboard quarter of the boat, giving it a most uncomfortable motion.

When the 18-mile run was finally over, Allen and Hero began

fishing off the Gypsum Reefs, near the south shore of the Virgin Basin, where underwater hilltops rise from a depth of 70 feet to within 10 feet of the surface. The wind rose. Allen, with his fearsome limp, was having an awful time just staying on the boat, even with the raised seat on the forward casting deck to steady him. The waves tossed the boat as the wind grew stronger. They lifted the thrashing trolling motor clear of the water. Balancing, even for the agile Hero, was like trying to stay on the back of a large bucking fish in the water.

Hero kept an eye on Allen, and every time he saw Allen's rod tip bend he called, "Fish?" Often as not, Allen would look bleakly back down the length of the boat and say, "Rock."

Allen caught seven nonkeepers, and each time Hero would say, with sympathy but not condescension, "Baby fish. Baby fish."

Hero, meanwhile, boated a 1.77-pound keeper to show for his day of bucking bronco fishing and terrifying runs across the plunging waves. "Harold was kind and a gentleman," he said when he reached the safety of the shore. "But I was afraid my bones would be broken."

Hirokazu Kawabe and Harold Allen were not the only fishermen affected by the wind. The sun-dazed anglers who had spent all day trying to keep their balance on the pitching boats looked like drunken sailors back on solid ground. They lurched as they came up the marina dock and the concrete walkway to the weigh-in. The fishermen who had deep-water fish found it impossible to work their baits effectively; the wind clawing at the light line removed all sense of feel, and the sometimes delicate nudge that indicated a strike was lost in the tremors of the line.

"It's mean out there," somebody said. Favorite Rich Tauber brought in one fish, and said, "If it calmed down, I could catch a limit."

But 225 tournament fishermen had produced only ten limits on the first day of the U.S. Open. Gerri Clunn stood under the striped awning that had been erected for sun protection at the top of the walkway and looked out on the raised stage where Rick's and Kotara's fish were being weighed. "I can't believe nineteen pounds of fish out of that one boat," she said. "That puts a lot of pressure on those fish."

She worried that Rick's fishing spot didn't have enough fish to last four days. And she knew that a spot that had produced the first- and fourth-place catches for a single boat would draw considerable attention. Rick had seen few fishermen in practice, and none today, but tonight, over dinner tables, between hands of blackjack and on room telephones, his location would be discussed, guessed at, and eventually pinpointed. Independently discovered, the spot would be fair game. Since nobody but Clunn had located these fish, the fishermen were honor bound not to snatch his spot. Clunn could give it up or invite others to fish the same area, but nobody could move in uninvited without committing a serious breach of tournament etiquette. As the tournament went on, however, an angler could find many ways to rationalize fishing near another: he might have planned it from the beginning; he might simply be trying a new pattern; he thought Clunn was moving somewhere else. There were also, of course, some fishermen who subscribed less fully than most to the unwritten codes of sportsmanship, and felt that ostracism was a small price to pay to win $50,000. Somebody might learn where Clunn was fishing and try to get there first. Clunn, too, was aware of these dangers, and he moved to protect his territory.

"My area's not really big enough for two boats," he told Jimmy Houston on the weighing stand. He served notice that he would fish the area again and that he expected others to stay out. In case somebody hadn't heard him, he repeated himself at the news conference later at the Tropicana.

"They're going to have to beat me there," he said when asked if he feared poaching by other fishermen. "It's a very small area. If they beat me there, then I'm going to go in, and if they'll move out, then I'm going to fish it. If they don't, then I'm going to have to move off and wait till they move. There are no boats around me right now. It's always possible [that someone could move in]; people change water every day, but I don't think anybody would do it intentionally."

This was intimidation on Clunn's part, and he followed with another intimidating ploy. It was great sport for questioners to ask the leading fishermen what baits they used to catch their fish, and listen to the various evasions. "One of those underwater baits," was a typical response. Clunn said he was fishing with "a perfect bait." Heads knocked all over the South Pacific Ballroom as fishermen leaned together to ask each other what they thought it was.

Clunn's perfect bait was, in fact, not a bait at all but a plastic jig and spinnerbait skirt. The Stanley Jig Company, one of Clunn's sponsors, planned to introduce the new skirt at the American Fishing Tackle Manufacturers Association tackle show and convention in Dallas in two weeks, but Clunn and a few others had prototype copies. The skirt differed from past models because it was translucent, with applied reflective flaking of various colors. This solved a problem for fishermen. Rubber skirts—like tiny hula skirts of rubber band–sized strips—had grown popular because they fell through the water with a natural motion and they could be made to be interchangeable. White and "chartreuse"—actually a lime green—were popular colors; in dark water they presented a light silhouette that was easy for the bass to see. There was no rubber skirt, however, that had a similar effect in clear water. Stanley's skirt, with its metal flakes that picked up light like sequins, did that.

Whether it was the perfect bait was arguable, but Clunn's announcement had the effect of distracting the other fishermen. Instead of concentrating on what they had to do to win, they now were worrying about Clunn and his invincible bait. And that meant, he felt, that they would beat themselves.

The draw that followed the news conference that Wednesday night paired Clunn with a tall, curly-haired fisherman from Tempe, Arizona, named Greg Hines. When she heard the name, Gerri Clunn felt a shiver of trepidation, for Hines had won the first U.S. Open in 1981. No one since had come close to equaling his winning weight of almost 50 pounds.

If Ricky has to share his fish with a strong fisherman every day, she thought, how long can they last? She felt almost resentful that he had drawn a strong partner for the second day.

The wind continued on Thursday. It blew like the Saharan hamrattan, casting a pall of windblown dust across Las Vegas. It blew 20 to 30 miles an hour, and gusted up to 40, and again the wind worked to Clunn's advantage.

From the start at Calville Bay, Clunn was eleven minutes from his fishing spot. He could start fishing earlier—important to his

pattern of morning strikes—than the fishermen who were running 25 or 30 miles, and return to the weigh-in in anything short
of a hurricane. The wind not only interfered with the way the
deep-water fishermen worked their baits; it reduced their fishing
time and kept them from moving easily from one spot to another.

The morning brought some clouds, and it was cool for Lake
Mead: the forecast high was 103°F. Most of the boats again turned
upstream when they left the Calville Bay Marina. All the signs
boded well for Clunn, except that the man in the boat with him
could help him decimate his fish.

Clunn respected Hines. Hines had not done that well yesterday, with 4.47 pounds, but he fished Lake Mead several times a
year and knew the water well. Clunn disciplined himself to concentrate on catching his five fish, and not to worry whether Hines
was catching his.

He nosed into the cove south of Saddle Island. Wind-driven
waves rose up under the boat and pushed it toward shore. Clunn
shut off the outboard and in a single motion shrugged off his life
vest and stood to move to the front of the boat. He lowered the
trolling motor into the water and pulled up the Velcro strap that
held his rods to the deck. He chose the one with the "perfect"
bait, the spinnerbait with the new Stanley skirt, and cast it among
the salt cedars at the head of the cove.

Randy Moseley had spent Wednesday with Jeff Munson nearly
40 miles from Calville Bay in the Gregg Basin, and returned to
the weigh-in shaking his head over his one, 1.36-pound fish.

"I should have had four," he said. "This hasn't been my year.
I don't know what's wrong. I lose too many fish and I don't know
why. I'm doing everything right. Last year I didn't lose many fish
at all. It's just one of those years."

By Thursday's cloudless dawn, however, Moseley had regained
his spirits. He said his tackle shop sponsor had wired $300 de-
spite the robbery. At the lake, he kept checking his watch until it
was eight o'clock in the central time zone, and then ran to a phone
booth to call Beebe Batteries in Missouri. He returned with a not-
at-all-firm promise of $500 and an elaborate plan, to be related to
Jean back at the hotel, for getting the money wired to the cage at
the Tropicana's casino. Now, as he and his partner, Dick Fulkerson

of Arizona, sat at the staging dock in Moseley's boat, smearing sunblock on their noses and making their last-minute lure selections, Randy predicted that he would rise into contention. "You could do it in this cove we're going to be fishing," he said. "Get a five-pounder out of there and then catch a limit, and we'll be right up there."

Moseley's optimism was seemingly unquenchable. But many held less sanguine views of his chances for success. Moseley was popular enough among the fishermen. He was unflaggingly helpful, and never hesitated to share any equipment he could spare. He never failed to stop to aid another angler whose boat was broken down or was in trouble. But the same qualities that made him popular meant he was not taken altogether seriously. Moseley's easy familiarity, his ingratiating manner, his confidence that was not always matched by his results, and the excuses that followed his failures, showed that Moseley was not sufficiently single-minded in his pursuit of excellence. "Too flighty," Rick Clunn had said.

By Thursday afternoon, Moseley's plight with his room had reached the ears of Don Doty, and the U.S. BASS president looked askance at Moseley's story. "Did you hear what he tried to pull with his room?" Doty demanded. "He's always trying to pull something."

It turned out that Doty's ire was due partly to Moseley's having questioned the tournament requirement that fishermen stay at the Tropicana. He had told Doty that the rule had cost the Open "forty or fifty" midwestern entries that could have swelled the tournament's prize purse, and Doty had not appreciated the interference.

"He'll never make it," Doty said scornfully. "This is a humbling sport," he added, implying that Moseley was not sufficiently humble or willing to face the consequences of his actions.

On the water below, the first boats were returning from the windswept lake into Calville Bay. On one side of the long dock at the foot of the hill, Nevada fisheries officers manned a bargelike tank in which the bass would be held once they were weighed. Some would be measured, tagged, and weighed again before they were returned to the lake, as part of a state conservation program. The returning fishermen went to the fisheries' boat for the bags they would need to carry their fish to the stage at the makeshift arena above. Roland Martin stood in the line of waiting fisher-men. Moseley had sought out Martin and was attempting to enlist him as a mentor. He hoped to work as a guide for Martin on Lake Okeechobee in the winter to come. Martin said Moseley was at a vital point in his career.

"It's a cruel fact," Martin said, talking about Moseley's efforts to find sponsorships, "that after three or four years, unless you do some winning, you're not going to make those deals. It's now time. He has to win. It's his only salvation at this point."

But things continued to go wrong for Moseley on as well as off the water. He and Fulkerson had made a pounding, tooth-jarring run of 20 miles from Calville Bay up the Overton Arm to Miner's Cove on the western shore. Randy missed a strike there, and thought it could have been the 5-pounder he had predicted might be in the cove. They next drove 5 miles farther north to a group of large, rocky islands called Ramshead, Gull, and Heron. They were fishing in the lee of Ramshead Island, protected from the blustery south wind, when Randy's trolling motor quit. Randy worked to patch the frayed ground wire as they drifted toward the pitching waves, and lost half an hour's fishing time. Then, the big motor started idling at high speed, clashing and grinding when Randy put it into gear, and refused to push the boat into a plane.

Before they limped back to the weigh-in, Randy caught one 2.09-pound bass on a Zara Spook off Ramshead Island. Fulkerson also caught a keeper off the island. Randy saw several 3-pounders at a last-minute stop before the weigh-in, near Beacon Island out-side Calville Bay. One chased the Spook on two different casts but refused to strike. The ineligible stripers, on the other hand, were at his bait all day.

Nonetheless, when Fulkerson mentioned to Moseley as they fished that he was competing in an upcoming tournament in the midwest, Moseley's remarkable confidence bubbled up unabated. "If it's at Lake of the Ozarks," he said, offering his help, "you've got it wrapped up."

Jean Moseley waited at the marina and worried. Gerri Clunn did, too. It was one of the commonplaces of the pro bass tour that the women waited and worried. They were most often at the summer tournaments, when the children were out of school.

Gerri Clunn had never, in Rick's twelve years of professional fishing, gotten up in the morning for a takeoff. She could manage, as she had this morning, to stir and offer a murmured "Good luck," as he moved quietly about the room, and then it was back to sleep. Later, she would join some of the other wives for breakfast, where they would gossip about the latest new young wives, like the one who missed a tournament because she was attending cheerleading camp. High school cheerleading camp! They would discuss the burdens of success, like corporate tax returns, accountants, and, worst of all, audits—the Internal Revenue Service couldn't understand that bass fishing was a business—and drink coffee late into the morning. But at the tournaments she attended, Gerri was an unfailing presence at the weigh-ins. No matter how many boats were returning to the shore, she could pick out her husband's and follow it to the dock with an eagle eye for signs of the day's fishing.

"This is the only time I do get nervous," she said, peering from the open-sided tent down toward the lake. The tent, raised on poles, stretched across the walkway leading from the dock, and shaded an area perhaps 30 feet square directly in front of the weighing stage. Tumbled rocks were part of the landscaping, along with yucca plants, and the stage was set between a pair of palm trees. Red-shirted U.S. BASS workers periodically added ice to the tubs of water that would keep the fish before they reached the weighing stand. Jimmy Houston was shouting into the microphone, and his shrill voice over the loudspeakers added noise to the tension and heat. "I feel weak. Just drained," Gerri said.

Rick's boat was at the dock now. A knot of people formed around the boat with two former Open winners, and Gerri took that as a good sign. From a distance of a hundred yards, she counted the fish Rick took out of his live well by counting the times he ducked to reach his arm into the tank. "That's three, and he's still digging." When Rick had ducked five times, an audible sigh of relief burst from her lips.

Clunn and Hines walked to the foot of the dock and up the long walkway. Clunn wore a long-sleeved shirt to protect his arms from the sun, but Hines wore short sleeves. They both had heavy bags, and the distortion caused by the water in the plastic bags magnified the fish and made them look enormous. Gerri snapped a picture with a small 35-millimeter camera.

Hines was first to the stand. He had five fish, and the scale showed 8.22 pounds. Gerri shook her head. "That really worries me," she said. "They're splitting up those fish again." Rick's catch, also a limit, was slightly better, 9.55 pounds. It moved him into first place by 2 pounds over a California fisherman, Wayne Carey. Kotara added just 3.3 pounds to his first day's catch, and dropped to fourth. In third place lurked Art Price of Arizona, a quiet, consistent fisherman who had finished well in the last two Opens. When Houston asked Clunn if his area would last, Clunn renewed his claim of sovereignty.

"I think they're good for one more day," he said. "I'm going to stay there all day again tomorrow. I want to make sure there's none left before I leave."

He left the weighing stand and bearded Don Iovino, burly and Mephistophelian, and one of the best western fishermen, walked up and shook Clunn's hand. "You're just goddamned awesome," Iovino said. "I'll carry your rods anytime."

While Gerri Clunn breathed her sigh of relief, Jean Moseley held her own camera and waited anxiously. "Where the hell is he?" she wondered, scanning the incoming boats. And soon Randy came walking up the dock.

Evalyn Duncan, the lucky lady, had by Thursday evening won three more $1000 jackpots at the slot machine. That made five. The bottles of champagne that accompanied every jackpot were crowding the dresser in her room, and credit was piling up in her account at the casino. The luck that Arkansas fisherman Keith Brashers, her first day's partner, had hoped would rub off on him was delayed, but powerful. Brashers had come to Las Vegas without a boat. He returned from Thursday's fishing with a 5.09-pound bass that was the day's big fish, and was awarded one of the lavishly equipped rigs parked around the edges of the ball-room.

The news conference that followed Brashers's big moment was concerned with Clunn's "perfect" bait. The outdoor writers covering the Open were curious about this new development that had placed Clunn in the tournament lead, and ignored the other tournament leaders to pepper Clunn with questions. What was it? Clunn wouldn't say.

"It's not a gimmick. It's not a miracle drug. And as my partners have proven, they didn't need it to go out there and do well," he told a questioner. "It's just an alteration of an age-old bait, is all it is. The key is still knowledge and working hard and confidence in yourself."

Clunn had been working hard. He made 10 casts every minute with a spinnerbait if he was covering the water the way he liked to, or 600 casts an hour. Deducting running time, time spent changing rods, and so forth, he might make as many as 4500 casts in a nine-hour day. A starting baseball pitcher might make 100 good pitches before weakening, with three days between starts. Gary Klein had said, "The champions will pace themselves, and if they're not exhausted at the end of the day, they'll count it as not trying hard enough." But at the midpoint of the tournament, lost sleep, heat, and dehydration were accumulating to rob Clunn of his edge.

"Fatigue becomes a factor," he said on Thursday night, sitting in his room and picking at a plate of fruit salad. "I'm getting used to the heat. But you get more tired every day, and you don't quite catch up. The first thing it affects is your concentration, your decision making, whether you should move."

He put down his fork and spread out his hands. They were furrowed with angry red line cuts, and other scars that must have come from handling fish. He flexed them painfully. "It affects your casting, how you hold the rod. It gets harder to close your hand." He bunched his hands slowly into fists, and opened them again. "But once you get out there, you're not even hardly aware of it," he said. He paused. "Even though I can see my grip is weakening."

That night, the wind that had helped Clunn simply by hurting the other fishermen, keeping them from moving easily from place to place and costing the deep-water anglers the feel of their baits in the water, was weakening too.

"That wind's really died down out there today," Gerri Clunn said when she reached Calville Bay on the afternoon of Friday, July 18. The small-craft warning flags were gone, and the flags and banners that had streamed from poles on the weighing platform now fluttered weakly.

The third-place man, Art Price, was first to the scales. Price,

with his bearded, smiling face, looked like a friendly college pro-
fessor, but there was menace in his inexorable consistency. He had
brought in limits the first two days. Now he had five more bass,
and they were good ones that averaged nearly 2 pounds each.
They gave him a three-day weight of 24.08 pounds. Clunn, who
was still on the lake, had started Friday's fishing 4 pounds ahead
of Price, but now that advantage was in question.

The pressure on Clunn had begun long before the weigh-in.
Early that morning, in the cove below Saddle Island, a weak breeze
still stirred the water, and the spinnerbait that had performed so
faithfully the first two days was good for one more fish. But that
was all. The south wind died with the rising sun, and the rough
water that dictated the spinnerbait was gone. Clunn started casting the Pop-R, which attracted more hits but hooked fewer fish.
The first bass hit the red-and-white chugger at 6:30, and he lost
it. Another hit at 6:40, and another at 7:00, and he caught the
second. At 8:30 he got a fourth hit, and lost that fish, too.

Other fishermen moved in. Clunn's 500-yard cove became
crowded with boats that kept the fish constantly disturbed. Clunn
had been making forty-minute passes through the cove, allowing the
fish that chased his bait to return to the bushes before he started
another pass. Now one boat after another was passing among the
salt cedar tufts, and the fish had no time to settle down and return
to cover.

With two fish in the boat, Clunn moved to a line of underwater moss beds that paralleled Boulder Beach 2 miles south of Saddle Island. Here he used the cigar-shaped Zara Spook. He hooked
and landed a bass at 9:30, and another at 11:00. At 2:30 in the
afternoon, he moved to the north side of Saddle Island and fished
without success until he left for the weigh-in. He returned to
Calville Bay with only four fish in his live well. His partner, Don
Sleight of California, had one.

"The lack of wind hurt me more than anything else today," he
told Houston as his fish were weighed. "I was keying on the wind,
and I had to change baits to catch what I caught. I had the strikes,
I just didn't execute as well."

Clunn's voice rasped with weariness. Gerri said, "He's tired.
I've got to put that boy to bed tonight at seven-thirty."

The scales showed 6.54 pounds. Clunn's lead had shrunk to
less than a pound, 24.98 pounds to Price's 24.08. It looked as if

Clunn's fish were giving out. Greg Hines moved into third. He had plenty of his fish left, he said, since he had caught Clunn's the day before. But Clunn insisted the spots he'd found in practice were good for one more day.

"I've just got to hook the fish, somehow, someway," he said driving back to Las Vegas and the Tropicana. "I didn't hook the fish today."

Houston kept poking innocuous fun at the Japanese fishermen. First it was the sushi joke, which he repeated at the Wednesday weigh-in. The names remained unpronounceable to Houston's Oklahoma tongue, and when he paired Japan's leading bass man, Masahiro Hiramoto, with Randy Moseley in the Thursday night draw, he said, "I'll just call him Hiro for short. But then they're all short," he added, giggling uncontrollably at his own joke.

The money Moseley expected from Missouri had failed to arrive, and late Thursday night, the hotel woke him with a phone call to discuss payment for the room. He looked tired and distracted on Friday morning.

At Friday's weigh-in, Moseley's relations with Doty took a turn for the worse. Moseley checked in a minute late, and he and Hiramoto were each docked a half-pound. Moseley ran around frantically checking his watch against every timepiece he could find, but Doty was inflexible.

"Well, Randy, if you were a professional fisherman, you would have made it in," he said over Moseley's protests. Jean said something under her breath.

On the weighing stand, Houston decided that Hiramoto—who wrote about bass fishing, hosted a fishing show on Tokyo television, and owned a company that produced handmade lures (one that he gave Randy was as delicate and luminous as a goldfish in a garden pond)—lacked a proper knowledge of English. "I want to teach you a good Southern word," he said. "Say 'bubba.'"

Hiramoto repeated the unfamiliar southernism haltingly: "Bub-Ba." Houston made him say it again.

Then Houston made Randy say it. "Bubba," Randy bellowed, laughing at the silliness of it all.

"OK, there you go. Bubba. Now you all can come to Oklahoma," Houston said.

Driving back to Las Vegas, Moseley and Hiramoto conversed

as best they could about their day together. They had fished far-
flung points in the Gregg Basin, in the Temple Basin just west of
Virgin Canyon, and in the Boulder Basin opposite Calville Bay.
Randy had weighed-in three fish, and Hiramoto two, and Randy
said, "I could have caught two limits if I caught every fish that
hit."

As it was, Moseley was out of contention, with 7.4 pounds after three days. Hiramoto was in fortieth place, with 9.91 pounds.
Moseley said he held out hope for a big string on the final day
that would lift him into the money.

Suddenly Hiramoto seemed lost in thought. He was quiet for
a moment, and then he looked at his companion. "Randy," he said.
He acted slightly embarrassed. "Randy, what's a 'bubba'?"

Clunn hoped for wind on the final day. So did Art Price. "Let
there be wind," Price implored at the news conference. A calm
day was forecast, but Clunn, always thinking, suspected the fish
might be fooled into believing it was a windy day. For it was a
weekend.

"The recreational boat traffic should have an effect similar to
the wind," he said. "It'll keep the water stirred up. That might
indicate a return to the spinnerbait. I'm kind of looking forward
to it."

Clunn also hoped for a partner "who doesn't fish me all day."
Sometimes being Rick Clunn was like being the top gunfighter in
a western town; partners would fish aggressively, placing their casts
on top of Clunn's, to try and show they could outfish the champion. "If he does, we'll have a confrontation. I won't sit there and
take it like I would normally," Clunn said. But Bob Porter, out of
Yuma, Arizona, had nothing to prove.

Clunn reached the lake before first light. When the others arrived they found him waiting, as they had each morning of the
tournament. He seemed at one with the earth and air and water,
integral to the scene and not apart from it. It was unnerving, as if
he had been there all night in some shamanistic ritual, painting
himself with clay and calling down a convergence of the elements
to perform his will.

The sun appeared clear and hard across the low mountain at
the entrance to the bay. Clunn turned south for the fourth day,

the thirteenth boat in the third flight of boats to leave. The earth stirred with the sunrise, and with it came a little wind. Clunn considered his options; a top-water plug would attract more hits, but the fish were less likely to be hooked; bass would hit the spinnerbait less often, but were more likely to wind up in the boat. He decided on efficiency, and cast the spinnerbait as he moved along the moss beds south of Saddle Island.

Clunn's early morning pattern held. The first bass struck the spinnerbait within minutes, and Clunn braced himself and reeled it in, lifting it into the boat without the net. There are two versions of what happened next. In Clunn's version, he took the hook from the fish's mouth and threw his rod in the water, deposited the fish in the live well, and moved to resume fishing before he realized that his rod was missing.

"Uh, I think you threw it over," Porter said carefully.

Clunn looked, and saw the spinnerbait hooked on the deck carpet, line trailing over the side of the boat. He hauled in the casting rod hand over hand. "Guess I'm more excited than I thought," he said.

Porter doesn't remember it that way. "I read that, and I don't know where he got that," Porter said later. "Maybe it happened earlier with one of the other guys he fished with. I'll tell you one thing, though. That guy is a fishing machine. Even making long casts with that spinnerbait, I bet he was making six casts a minute. He never let up."

Could Clunn have kicked the rod over by accident and retrieved it without Porter noticing? "No. I sure would have noticed something like that." Was it an apocryphal tale told to enhance Clunn's reputation? Most likely, it was a moment that transpired in deep intensity. By then, Clunn was fishing almost in a fugue state of concentration and exhaustion, in which memory is a tricky thing. If he could not remember everything that happened during the day, it seems equally possible that he remembered things that did not happen, but that he imagined.

Two more bass struck the spinnerbait, two more went into the live well, and it was still early. Then the wind died and the strikes stopped. The sun bore down and glittered off the water in the rising heat. Clunn moved to the other side of Saddle Island. It was still early, but Clunn had told himself that with Price and Hines behind him, he had to get a limit in order to win. Jet skis and boats pulling water-skiers began to zoom around the coves, and divers set out buoys, but Clunn was unable to coax more bass into striking the spinnerbait.

The night before, Clunn had been sleeping when Gary Klein called him. Klein was well down in the standings. He had heard Clunn talk about his pattern of early strikes, and he knew after yesterday that Clunn was not able to catch fish late. Klein offered his friend some advice: bass would hide in the clefts of vertical rock walls, where pockets of shade would keep them cool. They could be caught on spinning tackle and light line with lightly weighted, 4-inch plastic worms, baits Clunn called "California sissy baits," because they were so different from the fast, powerful lures he preferred. And so, at noon, Clunn put down his spinnerbait.

He drove to the north shore of Las Vegas Wash, where creviced walls plunged straight down into the water. Working from fissure to fissure along the sheer rock faces as time was running out, Clunn caught his fourth bass at two o'clock and his fifth 30 minutes later.

Some other things happened: Randy Moseley, with no fish, stopped to pick up Don Iovino, whose motor had blown, and returned him to the weigh-in with four big bass that moved him into fourth place.

Jean met the empty-handed Randy at the dock. They walked up the dock together, and Jean was remembering the Monday night when she had left Randy in the casino. "I was dreaming of you winning that $3200," she said. "I saw a leather jumpsuit and a black evening dress you would have loved." But what money they had had gone, finally, for the room.

Roland Martin said he hoped Art Price won the tournament. "I don't know why. Professional jealousy, I guess," he said.

An Arizona fisherman, John Murray, weighed-in and moved 2 pounds ahead of Clunn. Price had not returned.

The sun beat down and the desert wrung the moisture out of everything, but the air was laden with expectation. Voices sounded parched and dry. Gerri Clunn remained at the top of the walk under the tent. She was wearing a short cotton jumpsuit, white with pale green stripes, and her hair was pulled back in a pony-tail. She scanned the lake through her Porsche sunglasses, and resisted the urge to run down to the dock. The boats were coming in, disgorging weary fishermen, but Rick was not among them. She spied his boat circling slowly in the harbor. "They must have asked him to stay out there," she said, "...with no regard for the widow on the walk." Brooke and Cortney waited with their mother.

A short, stocky fisherman with a thick mustache and a rolling gait labored up the hill. Mike Dyess, a Montgomery, Texas, neighbor of the Clunns, had a report: Rick has four fish.

John Phillips, an Alabama fishing writer, updated the report a moment later: Rick has five fish.

The weigh-in droned on. Gerri tamped down her expectations. Art Price still had not weighed-in. Tournament officials were holding back Price, too, so that they could bring the two leaders to the scales together. They were squeezing as much tension as they could from the event. And the tension was mounting. Nobody coming to the scales could make a difference now, except for Price. Anything less than winning would be a disappointment, but Gerri refused to let herself believe that Rick had won. She searched for the right emotion to display: generosity in victory, or grace in defeat. One or the other had to be ready when Rick came up the hill.

Brooke, at 12, was less restrained. She ran downhill with her hands by her sides in a closed, cautious sort of way and joined the crowd that surged toward the two boats as they finally nosed against the dock. The crowd was too close for Gerri to see Rick taking his fish from the live well. After what seemed a long time, but was only a minute or two, Rick appeared with Brooke beside him, and started up the hill. Brooke could not walk. She ran, prancing and skipping and bounding, toward the tent.

"There's a girl who can't keep a secret," Gerri said. She couldn't help smiling, and Bill Bucher, the Mercury outboards representative, said, "Try to keep a straight face."

Brooke bounded across the rocks to where Gerri stood under the tent. She was all smile and braces, and long, coltish legs. "Mommy, Daddy's got a limit, and Art Price only has one." She said it as if it were a confidence, so that no one else could hear. As Clunn carried his bag of five fish under the tent to the weighing stand, people began to clap.

Price said, "I had three days worth of fish, and that's all. I needed that wind to blow, and it didn't do it."

Minutes later, Gerri, Brooke, and Cortney stood around Rick

on the stage. Jimmy Houston shouted questions, flash bulbs winked in the bright sun, and television cameras rolled. Photographers called for kisses. Clunn's 8.63 pounds had given him 33.61 for the tournament, more than 7 pounds ahead of Murray and 8 ahead of Price. Greg Hines finished fifth. The trophy Clunn held was half as big as Cortney. He handed it to her and she held it high for the cameras, struggling with its weight.

After all the congratulations at the weigh-in, after all the autographs had been signed and questions answered and pictures taken, there still were more pictures to be taken and more questions to be asked. Clunn returned to his boat and was directed to a corner of the cove near the staging dock. Gary Klein, anticipating the photo session, had thoughtfully kept a bass in his live well. Clunn fought it for the cameras until the exhausted fish had no more fight to give, as photographers clambered like bighorn sheep upon the rocks around the water.

The entire family was diverted to a bus full of outdoor reporters for the trip back to Las Vegas, while someone from U.S. BASS returned with Clunn's van and boat. Clunn stood at the front of the bus like a tour guide, and spoke into a microphone as he revealed his perfect bait and told of each day's fishing. Gerri closed her eyes and said, "You know that question, 'Are we having fun yet?' Well, now we're having fun."

That night, the dais in the South Pacific Ballroom was decorated with bundles and bundles of $100 bills, guarded by a large, unsmiling, balding man wearing an ill-fitting suit and a large pistol on his hip. Each of the top sixty finishers was introduced in turn, and each had someone to thank, so the banquet took awhile.

Clunn's face was sunburned outside the curve of his hat brim, and his blue eyes were bloodshot. He had forgotten to pack a tie; his shirt was open at the collar and he wore a tan linen-weave sport coat and light-colored slacks. He had invited the Open's youngest fisherman, 16-year-old high school student Jason Hackerd of Upland, California, to join him and his family at their table in front of the stage. Hackerd and his mother sat with the Clunns and watched the parade of winners on the dais. Finally, at nearly eleven-thirty, the time came for Clunn to speak.

His remarks to the weary anglers and their families in the room were brief, and along the lines that fishing had come to expect from Clunn. "We have the potential to be the greatest sport there ever was," he said, and pointed out young Hackerd as an example of what he meant. "This sport allows a 16-year-old, who has the aspirations of doing what I'm doing, to compete with fishermen at all levels. That's the beauty of the sport. And unlike other sports, tennis, golf, whatever, that eliminate you because of your age, because of your physical attributes, this sport doesn't. If we remember that, and treat the sport right by supporting conservation, we've got the ability to be the greatest of all sports."

During a last round of family pictures, Cortney held $50,000 worth of $100 bills, and tossed the bundle like a ball of wool. At the end she leaned her head against Gerri's waist and said, "I want to go home. To my real home."

Amid all the talk—the questions, answers, speeches, and heartfelt words of thanks—one query had gone almost unnoticed. It came on the bus with Clunn from Calville Bay back to Las Vegas. The reporters had finished with their questions and returned to quiet conversation. From the swaying, air-conditioned bus, the passing desert landscape seemed dreamlike and surreal, and everyone was drowsy from the hours and the heat. Clunn turned to a sportswriter from Chattanooga, where preparations were beginning for the Classic, and asked, "What's the fishing like now on Chicamauga?"

# The Classic

After winning $50,000 in the U.S. Open, Clunn felt the familiar tug of complacency. "After you've just won a big one, you think you don't deserve to win another one," he said. At the same time, he thought of winning the All-American, the Open, and the Classic all in the same year, a grand slam that had never been accomplished in bass fishing by one man. "If I have any strong urges, that's one of them," he said. "My mind keeps going back to putting them together." And Clunn owned the Classic, after all. After three wins, and second-, third-, and fourth-place finishes, he had not been embarrassed to incorporate himself as Clunn's Classic Enterprises. So he postponed his fortieth birthday party and went to Chattanooga.

He had recuperated for a few days first, sleeping much of the way back to Texas from Las Vegas while Gerri drove the van. He lolled around the house, watching Houston Astros baseball games on television, trying to empty his mind of the Open and focus ahead, to the Classic. Toward the end of the week, he hitched up the boat again. He reached Chattanooga on his birthday, July 24.

Clunn rarely "pre-fished" tournaments—going in to fish before the period during which the water was off-limits to contenders. He believed pre-fishing locked you into yesterday's conditions, blocking your intuition for what was happening in the water now. But the Classic was part fishing tournament and part command performance at interviews, parties, and dinners. The fishing days were short, there were just two practice days, and, said Clunn, there was "no time to make adjustments." He needed the extra time on the water. He spent five days on Chicamauga Lake, looking for bass along the milfoil lines. Other fishermen who saw him had trouble believing it was Clunn, because he was fishing practically naked, in the brief Speedo bathing suit Gerri had given him as an early birthday present.

By July 30, he had chosen two basic areas in which to fish. The same day, he started back to Texas. He had the big fishing tackle show and convention in Dallas to attend, and then he planned to "get things in order, my mind, my friends, my family. I want to get everything in order, and not have to think about anything else." When he returned for the Classic, Clunn said, it would be too late for "a cram course in focusing energy."

On Sunday, August 10, Randy Moseley entered Chattanooga from the west. His faded tan Vandura loped along Interstate 24 and into town from Nashville and Missouri. For the Classic fishermen, all but their tackle was provided: a glittering armada of special rigs meant they could leave their boats and vans at home and fly, with their wives, courtesy of B.A.S.S., to the tournament; hotel rooms, meals, and a smorgasbord of diversions were part of the package, from which nonqualifiers were excluded. But Moseley would no more have been able to stay away from the Classic than an addict from a fix. Moseley didn't drink, let alone use drugs, but he needed the high of being near the Classic, to drink in its heady atmosphere and be a part of it in any way he could. At the last minute, ABU-Garcia, his reel sponsor, had come along to help him satisfy his craving.

Randy and Jean had left Las Vegas the morning after the U.S. Open banquet, driving east to Albuquerque where Randy was to see his mother. On their way out of Albuquerque, before they were outside the city limits—thank God, thought Jean, they were not in the middle of the parched and lonely desert—steam boiled from the engine compartment into the van's interior. Randy, trying to save money when the engine was rebuilt, had not replaced the water hoses, and now they had burst. Jean pushed damp strands of hair from her forehead with the back of her wrist and thought that it was not the best vacation she had ever had. When the repairs were finally made, the Moseleys were behind schedule and poorer still.

A few days later, they were home at last and the call had come from Jim Kane, ABU-Garcia's vice president for marketing: Randy was a candidate for the ABU-Garcia pro staff. Kane offered a $100-a-month contract, $350 worth of reels, and $150 worth of logo-emblazoned clothing, and Randy accepted. He would be, in effect, a traveling salesman who received no commission and a pittance for a salary. The money was not as important to Moseley as the chance to be a part of the action. As a member of the pro staff, he would appear at seminars and outdoor shows to demonstrate and talk about his sponsor's reels. "Give me twenty-five young guys like this, who aren't looking to get rich but want to eat, sleep, and talk bass fishing, and I can keep this company going for another ten years," Kane said. ABU-Garcia, the merger of Swedish and American reel and tackle makers, had taken a booth at the Classic Outdoor Show, and Moseley was attending with his room expenses paid. He was booked at the tournament's headquarters hotel, the Holiday Inn in downtown Chattanooga. Moseley was under the same roof as the Classic competitors, but he could not anticipate the gap that lay between them.

The commercial flights into Chattanooga that Sunday were disgorging uncommon numbers of long, tubular packages. They came bumping along the luggage belt, stiltlike and ungainly, while the casually dressed, ruddy men waiting to claim them greeted each other with the fraternity observed among members of small, exclusive cliques. The packages held fishing rods.

Randy Blaukat waited for his rods and drew a breath filled with a sense of accomplishment and belonging. Two months ago he had been beside himself with worry until the final qualifying weigh-in, but now he was composed. The tic that had developed in his eye had gone away as soon as he had qualified. He was in the Classic, he had arrived at this pinnacle after a long and difficult professional season, and he was the only real rookie in the field, the only pro who had never fished a B.A.S.S. tournament before the year began. He would be fishing in the same field as Rick Clunn, his idol, and Roland Martin, Gary Klein, Larry Nixon, and all the stars of contemporary bass fishing. His career was on track; his interviews at the tackle show in Dallas had fetched him several sponsors.

Now, at the baggage claim, fishermen were talking all around him; their camaraderie enlarged the atmosphere. The moving belt brought a familiar piece of luggage into view, and Blaukat collected his big duffel bag with the Ranger Boats logo on the side, in which Shauna had packed the single red rose she always gave him before a tournament. He plumped the bag onto the floor beside him, next to the big tackle box. Shauna was a nutrition consultant; thanks to her, he was off junk foods forever. Waiting in vain for his box of rods to follow the duffel bag, Blaukat felt that, rods or no rods, nothing could go wrong.

Blaukat almost believed he could catch fish without a rod, so well had he done during his four days of unofficial practice earlier. He had been in Chattanooga at the same time as Clunn, staying at an "el cheapo" motel as he tried to divine the secrets of the fishing grounds. He had caught just three bass in three days on Chicamauga Lake, but one had weighed a monstrous 10 pounds. Then he had gone to Nickajack, the downstream lake, and caught a seven-fish limit in four hours.

"I found so many ways to catch a limit in Nickajack," he exulted in his flat southwest Missouri accent, giving a shy, boyish grin. "If I catch a three or four-pounder every day, I can win the tournament. If I'm leading on the last day, I'll stay in Nickajack and catch a limit. If I'm three or four pounds out, I'll go to Chicamauga and catch a big fish. I'm extremely confident."

Blaukat confided that before leaving for the Classic he had had the same dream three times. The last time he had it was the night before he left. In the dream, Blaukat was leading the tournament after the first day with a catch of 29 pounds and 8 ounces.

The rod box refused after some minutes to appear, and Blaukat left the matter in the hands of Ozark Airlines. Signs on the road from the airport to downtown welcomed fishermen to the 1986 BASS Masters Classic.

The Classic was supposed to have been in Memphis. Then somebody realized that a Shriners convention was scheduled in Memphis the same week and that all the rooms were booked. That was how Chattanooga had come to host the Classic, and why the Classic was being held on the same lakes as the Super-Invitational, two months apart. B.A.S.S. drove a stiff bargain when it brought a tournament to town: $10,000 was the rate for a regular invitational tournament, but the Classic was a font of publicity. Harold Sharp reckoned its value to the host area at at least $200,000, which is what the city and the state of Tennessee paid to strut their stuff before the horde of outdoor writers B.A.S.S. flew in for the event. A check to B.A.S.S. for $50,000 comprised part of the amount; the rest was found in the week of lavish entertainments and services provided for the anglers, their wives, sponsors, and the press.

No sooner had these participants arrived and registered, scooping up in the process free jackets, shirts, T-shirts, caps, and duffel bags, than they were mustered for the first event. At six that evening, they climbed aboard buses, rode into the country, and soon were disembarking for a ride back to town on a steam train dubbed the Evinrude Express for the occasion. Chattanooga can thank Glenn Miller and his version of "Chattanooga Choo-Choo," and the band of Union train thieves whose exploits were dramatized in *The Great Train Robbery,* for its renown as a railroad town, but its past has given way to new considerations; the train had just passed through a tunnel, with sooty ashes blowing nostalgically into the cars, when it stopped and the steam engine was traded for a diesel. The relic was barred from the city limits due to noxious emissions.

Ray and Susan Scott sat with Orlando and Carolyn Wilson on the train as it swayed toward Chattanooga. In the facing seats, Scott and Wilson talked and laughed like schoolboys. The two loquacious millionaires—Scott tall, deep-voiced, and hearty, with a way of sitting back and issuing pronouncements, and Wilson diminutive and agitated, energetic as a puppy—were thirteen years apart in age, but they enjoyed each other and increasingly kept company. The ideas they swatted back and forth sprung from lively, entrepreneurial minds. Wilson was describing his latest idea for a television show. "It's the world's greatest outdoorsman contest," he said, leaning forward in his seat. "There'll be canoeing, trapshooting, mountain climbing, backing a trailer,..."

"Well, I'll probably win that," Scott said. He would certainly win, he said, if the contest included chicken dressing. Scott announced that he could dress twenty chickens, exclusive of killing and plucking, in ten minutes.

"I don't believe it," Wilson said, and in an instant each man had taken $100 from his thick wallet and placed it against a future contest, rules, time, and place to be decided.

Roland Martin, another millionaire, sat in the same car. Martin had been Scott's companion in the early days of B.A.S.S., when they and a handful of other men were touring and trying to drum up memberships in the fledgling organization. Now, Martin was unhappy, not with Scott but with Wilson. Since halting the independent syndication of his television show to go with Wilson's Video Productions, Martin felt he had sacrificed control to become a glamorous front man. Martin's new boss had canceled a trip Martin had planned to the wilds of Canada to shoot his show, on the grounds that it was too difficult a trek, and now the purchase of an expensive underwater camera had been vetoed because, Martin was told, "everything looks fuzzy underwater anyway."

"I drive a $25,000 Suburban. I drive a $20,000 boat. I carry $2000 in my pocket. And all this over a $15,000 camera," the doleful Martin said, staring out at the exhausted August green of the drought-stricken Southern mountains. The sun was low, and shadows flickered on the windows of the train.

The train neared Chattanooga, and it occurred to Wilson that Scott might like to buy a railroad. He knew of one for sale, he said, a short line to a mill town. "Do you know what you can buy a diesel locomotive for?" he asked. "Fifty thousand dollars." The way he said it, it sounded like a bargain.

Wilson knew Scott had money to invest. Soon the rest of the bass fishing world would know it, too. For as the Evinrude Express followed the last mile of track into town, news releases were being distributed in the Classic pressroom announcing that Scott had sold his interest in B.A.S.S. Inc. The publishing empire Scott had built from a single tournament was now worth millions, and Scott owned 85 percent of it. "I'd look seriously at $25 or $30 million," Scott had said back during the spring at MegaBucks, although he'd said then that he wasn't interested in selling.

But, in fact, Scott was tired. He was not a manager, and he long ago had turned the business reins of B.A.S.S. over to its executive vice president, a cool, sharp-eyed woman named Helen

Sevier, who wore her gray hair short and dressed in tailored clothes. Sevier, 45, was a marketing expert who had been with B.A.S.S. since 1970. She had helped direct the expansion of its publishing operations to half-a-dozen outdoor trade and consumer magazines, the move into television production with *The BASSMASTERS*, and the growth in B.A.S.S. staff and membership. Now, said the press release, Sevier was heading a group of employees who, along with a Birmingham, Alabama, investor, had bought out Scott's interest in the company.

The news sent shock waves among the fishermen. Clunn, for example, suspected that Sevier was behind the move in 1985 to strip the Classic fishermen of their logo shirts, and guessed that she would continue to lean toward B.A.S.S. sponsors over those of individual fishermen. "She's on the side of the sponsors," Clunn said, "and that's not going to be good."

Sevier said the no-logo effort wouldn't be repeated, and pledged "business as usual" on the tournament circuit. Indeed, Scott remained head of the B.A.S.S. membership organization, and would continue in his role as front man, announcing the tournament weigh-ins, including the live broadcast on The Nashville Network planned for the Classic's final day.

Forrest Wood, the Ranger Boats founder and a courtly member of the old school, said Scott had moved bass fishing "from being whispered about in the backs of grocery stores to the front pages of sports sections, on television, and on the radio—a position it deserves among sports." That much was true. But Scott's sale of the company for an estimated $15 million (Sevier and the news release didn't say) meant the loss of something irreplaceable. It meant the decline of personal involvement in the sport, from a time when deals were sealed with handshakes to a time of concentration on numbers-crunching and the bottom line.

The next day, Sevier announced that Chevrolet, already associated with the Classic, would become the "official truck" of the B.A.S.S. tournament circuit, as part of a six-figure deal that involved advertising on *The BASSMASTERS*. A spokesman for the automaker said exposure among outdoor sports enthusiasts was the object of the deal. A fleet of identical small trucks was on hand to tow the Classic boats around.

*          *          *

Evinrude hosted Sunday evening's meal, and afterward Larry Koger, the Evinrude man in charge of special markets, presented navy-blue, logo-stitched blazers to the four Evinrude drivers in the Classic field. The presentation took Blaukat unawares; he had dressed for the heat, in a pair of tennis-length red shorts, and the blazer made a mismatched ensemble with his shorts and hairy legs. He was nonetheless a cordial presence on the stage, and he revealed his slightly awestruck first impressions of the Classic.

"If this is any indication of what the rest of the week is going to be like, it's gonna be great," Blaukat said. "It's not often you get to ride a plane, a train, and a bus,...all in one day," he added.

Gerri Clunn remembered Rick's first Classic, in 1974. It was the year he had started on the circuit, telling her he could make $40,000, and had won $1790 in five qualifying tournaments. The Classic was later then, at the end of October, and Gerri had returned to work full-time just the month before. Money was tight. She borrowed $500 to buy clothes for both of them, and outfitted Rick in a navy leisure suit with light-blue stitching and herself in pantsuits she no longer remembers. She felt for Randy, up on the stage in his shorts and blazer, and Rick understood the distractions the week held for the first-time qualifiers.

"It's like you're in a candy store, at first," he said. "People handing you drinks, big plates of food everywhere, sponsors, all the press. It's hard to concentrate, especially if you've never been exposed to it before. Then, as the week goes on, you turn your mind more and more to your fishing. It gets to where you get irritable about having to go to another cocktail party and another dinner. You just want to sit in your room and think about what you're going to do tomorrow." Clunn concluded that a fisherman could negotiate the Classic social schedule on automatic pilot, with, as he put it, "about ten percent of your mind."

At midnight, after Blaukat was asleep and coughing softly with the beginnings of a cold, his box of rods was delivered from the airport.

Monday, August 11, was "Press and Interview Day," and the fishermen bundled off to the Chicamauga Marina in a cool, drought-relieving rain for a three-hour photo session. Back at the convention center adjacent to the Holiday Inn, they sat like swamis in a series of booths arranged like stalls in a flea market, as the re-

porters went among them seeking wisdom. There were the thirty-
five qualifying pros, last year's champion, Jack Chancellor, and
five amateurs who represented the B.A.S.S. nationwide federation of bass clubs. Blaukat, as the youngest qualifier, attracted
much attention. A reporter with Chattanooga's Channel 12 TV
interviewed him, and Blaukat said, no, he wasn't intimidated fishing against the likes of Clunn, Martin, and Larry Nixon. "I've been
working toward this all my life," he said, "and I came here to win."

Blaukat's display of confidence was played back on the evening
news, and Amy Nixon, Larry's sun-freckled, brunette wife, pronounced him "a little strong-headed." She seemed to think Randy
should take his place at the end of the line. Many of the wives,
more than the fishermen themselves, expected displays of proper
humility among the younger qualifiers, as if their confidence disturbed the social order.

But Blaukat was undaunted. "I don't know what day it's going
to be," he said, "but one day I'm going to catch a twenty- to thirty-
pound string in Chicamauga. I'll know after practice whether it's
going to be the first day or the last day. I've just got a feeling I'm
going to win this tournament."

Tuesday, August 12, was the first day of official practice. Clunn
started fishing within sight of the dam on Chicamauga Lake, using the spinnerbait that had won the U.S. Open. He followed his
rumpled, heavily marked TVA contour maps. The maps located
freshwater springs, submerged buildings, old cemetery sites, and
other pre-inundation structure. But Clunn again concentrated on
the lines of milfoil grass, and soon switched from the spinnerbait
to a series of four crankbaits: his old favorite the Pop-R, a Bagley
"Balsa B" top-water lure, a Bagley diving crankbait called a "Kill
'R B," and a handmade bait he liked "because it throws well and
runs about the depth I want it to run."

Much had changed on the lake since June and the Super-
Invitational. The drought had dropped the water level and reduced its flow. The water was clearer than usual, and still, which
meant the fish would be less active. Tennessee Valley Authority
work crews were spraying the milfoil grass with an aquatic weed
poison. The spraying, done at the urging of the water-skiers and
sailors who also used the lake, had eliminated some productive

fishing grounds. Zell Rowland said the spot where he had won
the Super-Invitational had been sprayed, and with the loss of the
grass the fish were gone.

Where it was not sprayed, the milfoil had grown higher, and
in many places reached the surface, forming soggy sargassos that
stretched for hundreds of yards. Its gray-green tendrils looked
like leaves of asparagus fern. A boat could run through the patches
of grass without fouling the propeller, but casting into the milfoil,
Clunn inevitably reeled in to find wads of the sticky, clinging stuff
dangling from his hooks. He swatted the lures against the water
to remove the grass, and said that one of his objectives in practice
was to find a lure he could work close to the milfoil without fouling.

He concentrated on the two basic areas he had chosen on his
earlier trip to the lake, trying to "pinpoint productive areas within
general areas." He used the depth sounder to find 5- to 10-foot
water and seek out cuts, points, and breaks in the milfoil that were
likely to hold fish.

The early clouds loosened and scattered, gave way to a clear
sky, and later re-formed into a quilting of gray over the sun. Crows
called, harsh and mocking, among the trees at the edges of the
lake. A morning wind blew from the northeast, and later softened
to a breeze that brought a hum of cicadas across the water. Clunn
wore his usual long-sleeved shirt, but had put aside his shorts and
sandals in favor of navy slacks and a pair of canvas-and-leather
shoes. He always dressed up for the Classic.

Late in the morning, he had a run in which he caught six bass
in seven casts, but only one was the Tennessee keeper length of
12 inches. "That's what'll kill you in a tournament," he said. "All
the little fish that'll keep you from catching the big ones." Clunn
sought a bait he could work cleanly over the grass, but it also had
to be big enough to discourage the aggressive smaller fish.

"There are probably ten nonkeepers for every keeper in this
lake right now," he said. "That's going to be the key. Find an area
or bait that will allow you to improve your percentage of big fish
versus little fish."

At the end of the day he had caught just four small keepers
among a myriad of pipsqueaks.

*          *          *

Clunn did not fish late into the afternoon, as he liked to do, for the day was not for the fishermen alone to practice. The practice days were also dress rehearsals for the tournament weigh-ins, especially the Saturday weigh-in on live cable, for which the timing had to be just right. Scott already had told the fishermen to wait for a cue before transferring their fish from their live wells to the plastic carrying bags. "We can't have you bagging a big sack of fish while we're off the air in the middle of a commercial break," he said. So, at two-thirty, long before he would have stopped, Clunn returned to the Chicamauga Marina launching ramp.

The fishermen had left in the morning in three flights, fifteen minutes apart, and returned at midafternoon in the same sequence. Instead of going to the dock inside the marina cove, as they would have for a lakeside weigh-in, they waited at the launching ramp as one by one the boats were pulled out of the water by their tow vehicles. The fishermen and the reporters with them climbed into the trucks and sat back for a ride to the University of Tennessee at Chattanooga arena 5 miles away in downtown Chattanooga. The Classic weigh-ins were held indoors.

Harold Sharp had conceived the indoor weigh-in twelve years before, during a fit of worry in the middle of the night. The Classic in 1974 was at Joe Wheeler Lake in Alabama, and the October skies were ominous. Sharp got out of bed at two o'clock on the tournament's first morning, and walked to the dock where the Classic boats—even then the anglers fished from identical rigs—were tied up in a row. "I got to thinking what would happen if a storm came through and sunk all the boats," Sharp said, "and that was when I thought of indoor weigh-ins, so the boats would be out of the water and safe in case of a storm."

In 1981, after Sharp had figured out that live wells and holding tanks would keep the fish alive, the first indoor Classic weigh-in was held at the Montgomery, Alabama, civic center. By then, the purpose of weighing the fish in an indoor arena had to do less with protecting the boats than with encouraging an audience, for Scott had hit on the notion of promoting an outdoor show in conjunction with the Classic. The last day of the 1985 Classic at Pine Bluff, Arkansas, had attracted a standing-room-only crowd of 7500 to the Pine Bluff Convention Center, and more had clamored outside to be let in. The UTC arena was larger still, and Scott and Sharp hoped to fill it.

The trailered boats left the lake in a ragged convoy and followed the Tennessee River south to town on the Amnicola Highway, turned onto a surface street, and swung out for a sharp right turn into a drive that entered the floor of the hatbox-shaped arena. Across the street, a large yellow-and-white-striped tent was being erected for overflow displays from the Outdoor Show. Randy Moseley had become a laissez faire exhibitor; he had parked his boat at the curb with a "For Sale" sign taped to its side. His memo bill was not due for six months, but he thought it would not hurt to test the water.

The fishermen and their press partners returned to the boats for the grand entrance into the arena. Perched in the boat seats like riders on a parade float, they were pulled through a wide service door into a tight circle marked off with drape-hung pipes. Steep tiers of seats encircled the floor. The weighing stand, where Ray Scott was practicing his timing, had been fashioned atop a bass boat. Beyond the inner circle that included the weighing stand and press and camera areas, the Outdoor Show displays were taking shape.

The press anglers were weighing fish on the first day of practice; a $1000 prize, split between the reporter and the fisherman, was awarded for the biggest press bass caught each day. The fishermen were weighing only tackle boxes. They were limited to five rods and a single tackle box for the Classic, and the tackle box could weigh no more than 24 pounds. Orlando Wilson had not had time to pack his own tackle, and the assistant delegated to do it had called Rick Clunn for his advice. Now, Wilson's box was over the maximum weight, and Scott and Sharp were pulling handfuls of tackle from the box and putting it aside.

"Hey, wait a minute," Wilson howled.

Sharp kept digging out lures, plastic worms, and sinkers, but the tackle box remained too heavy. Finally Sharp, triumphant, reached into the bottom of the box and pulled out a large brick. Wilson mopped his brow and dissolved in laughter at the practical joke.

That evening's entertainment was just as ludicrous. The party assembled for a luau that began with a sumptuous buffet and ended with a hula exhibition. Fishermen with gray beards and drooping mustaches, and with considerable bulk, rolled their pants legs up above their cowboy boots and donned grass skirts to dance along with a professional troupe. They looked like the elephantine ballerinas of a Disney cartoon, and somebody called out above the music, "Anybody got a Weed Eater?"

A helicopter observed the beginning of the second practice day. Its rotors beat the air over the takeoff site, while a cameraman sat in its open door, sighting down at the fishermen in their boats. Randy Blaukat waited for his flight to start, and said over the roar of the hovering machine, "This is quite a change from fishing farm ponds with a spinnerbait four years ago."

Blaukat had fished around Joplin from the time he was 10, first on farm ponds, then on rivers, and then on a local lake, Grand Lake. He fished from an aluminum boat with a 9-horsepower motor bought with money scraped together from odd jobs. "I wanted to compete," he said, "but until two years ago I didn't have the money."

When the other kids in Joplin were cruising Main, or driving over the state line to Galena, Kansas, to drink beer and dance at Sgt. Pepper's, Randy was sneaking onto private farm ponds. He and his friend Tom Fitzgerald would catch seventy and eighty bass a night. It was with Fitzgerald that Blaukat started the Parkwood High School Bass Club. Bowling was Blaukat's other passion; he carried a 205 average in the Men's Ozark League for five years, and had applied for a Professional Bowlers Association card before he chose bass fishing. Until three years ago, Grand Lake had been the only lake he'd ever fished.

He made up in intensity what he lacked in experience. He took his cues from *BASSMASTER* magazine and the stories on Rick Clunn. "It gave me some guidelines to go by. I had no role models as far as tournament fishermen were concerned. I sort of adopted Clunn's attitudes, not only in my fishing but in my personal life as well." That meant, he said, that he tried to keep the demands of fishing and outdoor life in perspective. In listing their hobbies for the Classic program, most of the fishermen wrote "hunting" or "fishing" on the questionnaire. Moseley, after Justin was christened, had not known the denomination of the church. "I don't keep up with churches. I fish too much," he'd said. Clunn listed his hobbies as "family and friends."

But Blaukat departed from Clunn in his approach to the Classic. Clunn had never fished Nickajack Lake and didn't plan to. "From what I've seen, it could be won down there. I just don't like to gamble with those locks," he said. Blaukat thought the downstream lake represented his best chance to win the tournament. He had contributed to the $200 fund Jimmy Houston was collecting for the lock tender to assure a favorable schedule of openings and closings. He had had six keeper bites there during the first practice day, and he locked through to Nickajack at the beginning of Wednesday's practice session. Nine other fishermen and a camera boat from The Nashville Network joined him in the lock.

Blaukat blasted out the lower end of the lock and downriver until he reached a sweeping right-hand bend, where he stopped the boat and began fishing near fallen logs at the water's edge. "Lay-downs," or "fall-downs," the fishermen called the fallen timber, which were among the protective cover likely to hold bass. He was trying only for bites, and had bent closed the hook on his spinnerbait. Just before nine o'clock, a 13-inch bass managed to get hooked anyway, and Blaukat closed the hook some more. He wanted to establish that the lay-downs were among the places he could go to catch a limit, but after two hours and only the one strike, he said, "I don't think I can do it."

Driving downriver past Chattanooga, he entered a small creek on the right side of the river. The creek mouth was shaded with overhanging trees, but a short way beyond it was choked with fallen trees. Blaukat gunned the boat over one obstacle after another until he entered open water in a muddy, algae-laden slough that the river charts called Baylor Lake. It was an unattractive piece of water, 2 feet deep, covered with scum, and dotted with discarded tires. Blaukat dropped his portable pH meter in the water, and it recorded an abnormally high alkaline content. "But there's shad here, and current," he said, scratching his head and looking around. Then he realized the meter wasn't calibrated. He ducked and steered through a 10-foot-wide concrete culvert into an even smaller backwater, and finally gave it up to return to the main river.

"I wasted my time coming in here," he said. "But you have to do it. It could just as easily have opened up into a beautiful little creek back there, clear water, and six, seven feet deep. You never know."

It was as difficult to leave the slough as it was to enter it. With the big engine overheating and a warning horn tooting at full blast, Blaukat crashed over submerged obstacles and ignored the tree limbs clawing at the boat's side. "I take good care of my boat out of the water," he said. "But when it's in the water, I go hard. It's your living, you know? I don't let anything stop me."

At the end of the day, Blaukat struggled with ambivalence. He could not decide whether to fish Nickajack for a limit of small fish, or Chicamauga for scattered big ones. Most of the fishermen thought it would be the other way around, that the big fish would be caught in Nickajack and that Chicamauga would produce more of the smaller bass. Blaukat decided on indecision. "There's a hump just above the lock that I'll fish while I wait for the lock to open. If I can catch three keepers there, I'll stay in Chicamauga. Otherwise I'll go to Nickajack." His recurring dream was on the eve of being tested, and he felt a quickening urgency about its coming true.

Back at the UTC arena, drivers wheeled one after another into the tight circle by the weighing platform and discharged their passengers. B.A.S.S. workers transmitted instructions over walkie-talkies, and waved their arms like traffic cops as they ushered the vehicles into the spotlight on the arena floor. Randy Moseley watched from outside the blue-draped demarcation line, the Berlin Wall that separated the competitors and press and B.A.S.S. officials from the exhibitors. He had his usual smile and cheerful greeting, but his chin was tucked down against his chest and something about him looked forlorn.

Blaukat went over to say hello. They talked about the day's fishing, and then Moseley said, "Well, why don't you stop down to the room tonight? We're right down the hall from you, and I can show you some places on the map you ought to try."

"I don't know," said Blaukat. "You wouldn't believe how tight they've got us scheduled. Seems like every minute's taken up. I'll try to make it, but it'll be late." After a few minutes, he rejoined the fishermen waiting for the buses to return to the Holiday Inn.

Moseley said, "It's tough, you know? You fish with these guys all year, and you come to help out in any way you can, and suddenly it's you and them."

Indeed, all of the Classic activities were restricted, even the daily

news conferences at the convention center. Once competition started, the standings would dictate the participants. On that Wednesday before the tournament began, a young man from Marlboro,
Massachusetts, was asked to talk about how it felt to be an amateur
fishing with the pros. Danny Correia was the B.A.S.S. federation's
eastern division representative. He would join Roland Martin, in
his fifteenth Classic, Hank Parker and Larry Nixon, who each had
won a Classic, and Rich Tauber. Correia was flattered to be asked,
but he was nervous.

In many ways the amateur's route to the Classic from the federation is more difficult than the professional's gauntlet of six qualifying tournaments. A federation angler first must make his state
team in a series of weekend tournaments. Then his state team must
win a regional tournament, and he must be the top fisherman on
that team. Correia had won his ticket to the Classic the previous
fall, on New Hampshire's Lake Winnepesaukee, when he caught
32 pounds, 8 ounces of bass to lead Massachusetts over teams from
eleven other northeastern states.

It is somewhat misleading to refer to the federation fishermen
as amateurs. They do not reach the Classic by way of the invitational tournaments, but that does not prohibit them from fishing
those and other tournaments, and winning money. Correia, for
example, had fished the Super-Invitational as a prelude to the Classic, and finished 173rd. He later returned to Chattanooga for two
more weeks of pre-practice fishing. When he visited the local tackle
stores, the men behind the counters would ask him if he was fishing the Classic. He would say yes, and they would listen to his New
England accent and appraise him according to his youth and whether
they recognized his name. "Bet you're from the federation," they
would say dismissively.

He fished every day for those two weeks. On the first day he
caught three bass, and on the second day, three more. On the third
day, fishing with a person who knew the waters, he caught twelve
bass. During one stretch he made three casts, and caught a 5-
pounder, a 4-pounder, and a 3½. From that day on, Correia felt
he had a good idea where fish were to be found for the Classic.

Still, he was nervous about the news conference. Even Tauber,
like Correia a Classic rookie, was an experienced communicator,
and Martin, Nixon, and Parker had fielded thousands of ques-

tions. Danny had never been to a news conference before. He wondered what he would say.

If Danny Correia had not caught a bass the entire tournament, he would have been remembered for that news conference and the infectious excitement he discharged into the room full of 200 people. He was compact, 5 feet, 10 inches tall, and lean, about 150 pounds, from the construction work he did for his uncle when he wasn't fishing. There was about him a tautness like that of a spring toy, where you expect something to jump out and make you laugh. His red Fleck baits cap had an odd, high-domed look that somehow went with his jittery enthusiasm and the edge of near-panic in his voice. His voice! People make much of Southern accents, but in Chattanooga that afternoon they were suddenly hungry for the sound of Massachusetts, those broad Kennedy vowels with the "h" on the end. Danny was talking about the luck he'd had in practice—"a keeper, and I caught some shorts"—when Parker, 6 feet, 2 inches tall, and 200 pounds, with a Carolina accent that flowed slow as sorghum molasses, rose and shambled over to join him at the microphone.

"If y'all need for me to interpret, I'll be glad to do that," Parker drawled. "A show-aht is a nonkeeper."

"Oh, Gahd, where was I?" Danny said when the laughter died, and it started again.

Somebody in the audience asked him if he was intimidated fishing against legendary fishermen like Martin, and how he managed to overcome his awe in order to fish. His answer was felicitous.

"To be honest with you, I'm a nervous wreck up here," he said. "Every day I go out there, I feel like going around with paper and pencil and getting autographs. But I try to think that I made it here, and that means something. And I'm just going to give it my best, and have fun and try to catch some fish. They're nice guys, they're all just like you.... That's what everybody keeps telling me, anyway." That broke up the crowd again, and when Correia left the microphone he sat down to laughter and generous applause.

That night's program began with a trip to the Civil War battlefield at Chicamauga, Georgia. After young men in period clothing gave a demonstration of musket fire, Rick and Gerri Clunn walked over to Correia. Clunn laid a hand on Danny's shoulder and said cordially, "If you weren't a nervous wreck, I was going to be P.O.'d, because I was, the first few times I had to do it."

As it turned out, Correia's first news conference at the Classic was not to be his last. And from then on, only the leaders were on stage.

On Thursday, August 14, the first day of competition, the fishermen left the Holiday Inn in buses at six in the morning, carrying their rods and tackle boxes and dodging each other's rod tips. Some joked and laughed, others were polite, still others withdrew into deep thought. Among the young Classic rookies, Blaukat and Tauber were outwardly calm; Correia was agitated, drumming his feet on the floor. The buses stopped at a parking lot opposite the UTC arena, where the boats were lined up in a neat row waiting to be hitched and pulled to the lake. The trucks backed against them and pulled away, once the fishermen and their press partners were aboard.

"Today's your day, buddy," Correia's driver said, turning north against the inbound morning traffic.

"I'm trying not to think about it," he replied.

A crowd of 200 milled around the launch site. The fishermen and reporters climbed into the boats to be backed into the lake. Flashbulbs popped and winked when Clunn, Martin, and the other better-known fishermen reached the top of the ramp. Fans called encouragement: "Good luck, Rick." "Go get 'em, Roland." Word of Danny's performance at the news conference had spread, and a few people wished him luck. The trucks backed down the ramp until the trailers were submerged, and the boats backed into clear water to await their starting times. There was no wind. The water was flat and unruffled. The early sun was hot in a clear sky, the helicopter a clattering shadow swooping overhead. The first start was at seven o'clock.

For the Classic, Scott did the starts the old way, as virtual drag races among the boats in each flight. There were fourteen boats in two flights and thirteen in the third, fifteen minutes apart. Waiting for his flight to start, Correia idly trimmed his motor up until the propeller was out of the water. He caught his error and said, "Nerves. I had my finger on the trigger and I didn't even know it."

Scott stood in his boat and offered a prayer: "Give us a good day of fishing, and bring us all home safe and sound, in Jesus' name. Amen." Then, with the boats side by side in a rough line, Scott waved his Stetson and the tournament began.

Correia had found his fish in Nickajack and would lock through to the lower lake. But minutes remained before the lock opened, and he raced toward a spot 2 miles north of the dam and began fishing a buzz bait very fast over an old road bed. He made eighteen casts, had ten hits, and caught a nonkeeper before lifting his trolling motor and running for the lock. It opened promptly at seven-thirty, greased by the $200 the fishermen had pooled. Seven other boats, including Blaukat's, entered, a horn sounded, and the massive gates swung slowly closed.

Sluggish, ephemeral mayflies clung in clusters to the upper walls of the lock. The water dropped steadily down the algae-slathered walls, and the sky narrowed to a rectangular slot; it was a 49-foot drop from the upper to the lower lake. When the gush slowed, each fisherman loosed his mooring line and jockeyed toward the lower gate. They moved into position, and suddenly, without realizing what was happening, Danny was squeezed against the right side of the lock with nowhere to go. The gates opened and the boats roared out, some of them cracking against one another and then yawing and swerving in each other's wakes and spreading out to find smooth water. Danny was last out of the lock. He hunched down behind his windshield, pushed the throttle as far as it would go, and kept it there until he had passed every boat and reached the lower end of the lake, 40 miles away. He made his first cast at 8:30.

The fishing was slow for three hours. No, it was dead, nonexistent. Danny fished top-water baits along the edges of thick forests of milfoil grass in a spot called Rankin Cove. Then he switched to plastic worms, alternating with the top-water lures cast over the milfoil. Carp and drum lolled at the edges of the grass. Danny fished quickly and decisively, wasting no time either casting or moving from one spot to the next. Now and then he did the illogical things fishermen do to ward off despair, like calling, "C'mon, fish, where are ya?" The August heat rose, clouds moved without effect across the sky, cicadas began their steady rasping. The old slope-shouldered Appalachian hills rose soft and green a polite distance from the water. A long freight train moved along a causeway and snaked out of sight. Danny removed his warm-up pants and jacket. He stepped out of his tennis shoes and took off his cap, and fished barefoot and capless in navy shorts and a red shirt, hand-stitched with his name. "I think I'm going to have to work hard for these fish today," he said.

The morning passed and his window of time narrowed. The lock would open for the return to Chicamauga at 1:45 p.m., and it would take forty-five minutes to run back up the lake. At 11:25, with no fish in the live well and discouraged, Correia decided to fill his gas tanks and head upriver to another fishing spot. He stopped a hundred yards from Hale's Bar Marina to try a blue-flaked purple worm in a promising patch of milfoil grass. At 11:30, he landed his first fish.

It was an ugly patch of grass for one so prolific. The soggy, gray-green milfoil held cans and paper cups in its coagulated grasp. Danny guided the boat along the outer edge of the patch with one bare foot on the trolling motor's pedal controls, at the same time leaning out over the gunwale of the boat and plunking the weighted worm into the grass. At the first fish, he said, "I feel better. Now I don't have to get up in front of a thousand people and say, 'No fish.' At the second, another 14-incher, he exhibited a grin. The third was short enough to measure, but it made the keeper length. He snatched the fourth out of growth so thick the fish landed in the boat with a weedy topknot on its head. "Whoo-oooh!" Danny yelped. "Is it time to panic yet? How many's that? Four? I need three more."

He broke to run to the marina, where he was in such a hurry to return to fishing that his trembling fingers dropped one of the boat's gas caps in the water. Returning to the patch of milfoil, he worked along the inner edge, closest to the marina. When he caught the fifth bass, he muttered, "Two more fish, two more fish, two more fish." He caught the sixth, the biggest yet, at twelve-thirty, and pumped the air with his fist like Jimmy Connors after hitting a winning passing shot. Correia was breathing fast and having trouble putting a new worm on his hook. "Fuckin' can't stop shaking," he said. "Man, he hit it like a ton of bricks." He threaded on the worm, and dunked the hook back into the water between breaks in the milfoil, saying "C'mon, number seven, I know you're in there. It'll only hurt for a minute. C'mon, fish, hit me." Around him on the bow, drying shreds of the water grass littered the deck. Now he was repeating, "One more fish, one more fish."

He fished past one o'clock, pushing his time limit for returning to the lock, but he didn't catch another. The six he had brought low whistles of surprise from the men orchestrating the entrances of the fishermen into the arena, and they muttered over their walkie-talkies with the weigh-in officials inside. "You're leading the tournament, then," said Mike Runnels, who was relaying the catch reports. Danny broke into a grin of disbelief. He rubbed his hands together and tapped his feet. "Anybody got any clean underwear?" he said.

Danny's fish weighed 8 pounds, 8 ounces, and when he weighed them he was indeed the Classic leader. His weight was good for fourth place at the end of the day. "Sooner or later, we're going to be wiped out by one of these federation boys," declared Scott to the weigh-in crowd. "I never thought it would be somebody from Massachusetts, though."

In the lock returning to Chicamauga, Blaukat had caught Correia's eye and raised his eyebrows inquiringly. Danny held up six fingers, and Blaukat raised his eyebrows higher. Correia raised his eyebrows in return, and Blaukat held up one finger.

"I could have weighed-in four bass today if I'd caught all my keeper bites," Blaukat said after ending the day in thirty-first place with 1 pound 6 ounces. There were better-known fishermen behind him, including last year's champion, Jack Chancellor. Five fishermen had caught nothing at all, including Jimmy Houston and Hank Parker. But Blaukat, who had broken a line on one fish and a rod on another, was hardly satisfied.

He had been the first to leave the parade of speeding boats down Nickajack, stopping to fish around concrete bridge pilings where he thought bass would move to seek shade as the sun rose. "I should have spent twenty-five minutes doing that, but I spent almost two hours," he said. "Then I spent an hour on places I'd never been before, but I thought they'd be productive. I spent too much time jacking around today. I didn't use my time wisely. I need a big string tomorrow. I'll either get a big string or a goose egg."

Clunn was in the middle of the pack. He had caught just three small bass that weighed 3 pounds, 3 ounces. He said, "I caught my third keeper at eight-forty, and I thought I was going to have a good day." He planned to leave the main river channels he had been fishing, and go to a secondary area he had found in pre-practice.

"This thing can still be won easily with a big string. There's not anybody out of it," Clunn said.

Roland Martin led at the end of the first day. "He's been jinxed for sixteen years," said Scott, referring to Martin's history of frustration in the Classic as he brought him to the weighing platform. But Martin said at the news conference that his Classic jinx might have ended the previous evening. "Last night I was going through the lobby," he said, "and this little girl here at the Holiday Inn said, 'Mr. Martin, I've been watching you for years.' She said, 'Would you carry this little rabbit's foot for me? Be sure to put it in your pocket.' And I had it in my pocket all day, and I'm going to carry it for the next two days." He held up a red-dyed rabbit's foot on a key chain.

Martin's first-day weight was 10 pounds and 4 ounces. "This tournament's going to be one of ounces," he predicted.

Blaukat was an honoree at that night's banquet. He, Tauber, and Joe Thomas were introduced among the new members of the Du Pont Stren Line team. The convention center banquet hall was full to overflowing, and Jimmy Houston, the guest of honor, was awarded a check for $2500 for winning Angler of the Year. While B.A.S.S. attached no cash prize to the title, sponsors like Stren were making it increasingly worthwhile. When Houston was Angler of the Year in 1976, Stren awarded him just $500. Roland Martin estimated he had received a total of $17,500 from all his sponsors for the nine Angler of the Year titles he had won between 1971 and 1985. But now Mercury Marine was offering $5000 to each year's winner, and doubling the amount for fishermen who ran its Mercury or Mariner outboards. Choo-Choo Customs, the Chattanooga van conversion company, gave the winner a new tow vehicle. And other companies, as well, were recognizing the advertising value carried by the title, and sweetening the pot for fishermen who used their equipment to win it.

From Martin's standpoint, the Angler of the Year was just beginning to receive the attention he deserved. He saw it as a test of

consistency versus luck, and he was rankled by the attention given
the Classic winner versus Angler of the Year. "There has never
been any consistency in the Classic," Martin had said three years
before. "I don't like to use the word luck, but what it boils down
to is the people who win the Classic are people who just take advantage of a situation at the time."

Martin nonetheless had not turned down the lucky rabbit's foot
from his admirer, and he admired Clunn's prowess in the Classic
and other showcase tournaments, even as he was frustrated by it.
"I don't know how he gets up for the big ones and not the other
ones. It perplexes me," Martin had said after Clunn had won the
U.S. Open.

Clunn, meanwhile, was as perplexed by Martin's steadiness as
his rival was by Clunn's big tournament performances. Clunn long
had maintained that Angler of the Year was not so much a test of
skill as it was of information gathering, while the Classic was a test
of a fisherman's ability to adapt to specific conditions. He believed
Martin's success could be attributed to the extent to which he pre-
fished and talked with local guides, and believed Martin had failed
in the Classic because in its early years the location was a secret
and Martin was robbed of his ability to canvass for good fishing
spots. After 1977, when the fishermen had advance notice of the
Classic site for the first time, Clunn thought Martin simply wanted
to win so badly that he choked.

But now Clunn found himself attracted, although he steadfastly
denied an interest in the title. "I still can't get excited about winning
Angler of the Year," he said. "I don't know if I've deprogrammed
myself for it or what." He said his goal was the consistency that had
eluded him thus far in his fishing career. Consistency such as Martin
had exhibited. Consistency would be a gauge of Clunn's intuitive
thinking. It would mean that his ability to harness his mind was growing, that perhaps the perfection he sought was not unattainable.

"I'd like to not gear up and gear down, but to maintain consistency," he said. "I want to try to mentally prepare myself for
every event the way I have historically for the major events."

Underlying Clunn's thinking, despite his protests to the con-
trary, were the new rewards and attention attaching to Angler of
the Year. "It's starting to be worthwhile," he said.

*        *        *

While Blaukat was being welcomed to the Stren team in the crowded banquet hall, Randy Moseley was upstairs getting ready for an evening with his ABU-Garcia sponsors. Preparing to step into the shower, he confronted a shortage of clean towels. Naked from the waist up, clutching a towel around him, he opened the door to find a service cart and a maid just outside the room. The maid took one wide-eyed look at Moseley's hairy back and shoulders, and before he could ask for another towel she said, "Lord, honey, you must be a werewolf. I believe you're transforming."

Moseley related the story with a laugh the next morning. He used it to show the gulf, in terms of respect, between the Classic fishermen and the nonqualifiers who were there promoting products at the Outdoor Show.

The ABU-Garcia display was set up with the displays of several other tackle and marine companies off the floor of the UTC arena, and an interior hallway that encircled the arena led to more rooms and more displays. The Daiwa booth had posters of the baseball (Willie Stargell), basketball (Larry Bird), and football (Joe Montana and Nolan Cromwell) players who had endorsed its rods and reels, a campaign that had caused Clunn to wonder indignantly what Joe Montana knew about fishing. Down the hall in the same room as the large Mercury Marine exhibit, a jewelry manufacturer touted its gold and silver rings in breathless terms:

"The fighting fury of the largemouth bass, exploding from the water, may be the greatest sporting moment known to man. Now the excitement and thrill of that moment has been captured and transformed with unmatched attention to detail." A buyer could choose a ruby or a sapphire "in the eye of the tournament winning largemouth bass," for $319.95 in gold or $149.95 in silver.

Window shoppers wandered among the displays as the hour of the weigh-in approached. They handled the demonstration rods and reels with expressions of delight. A man picked up one of the ABU-Garcia outfits and hefted it. The Ambassadeur reel was graphite, like many of the modern casting reels on display at the Outdoor Show. Like most of the others, it was teardrop-shaped, compact and solid, as satisfying in the hand as an oiled firearm. Its matte black finish advertised an attention to function, and the smooth clicking of its meshing gears sounded happily precise; dials, knobs, and a quick-change spool feature pointed to versatility.

Beyond the powerful outboards, the electric trolling motors, the sonar depth sounders, and other electronic gadgets, the reels on display were as good a place as any to find advances in technology and precision manufacturing that have transformed fishing and its gear. The man cranked the reel handle and flipped the hookless jig sidearm down the aisle. "Whoo, that is smooth as mother's love," he said with reverence. "Boy, that is Jim Dandy to the rescue."

Moseley and another young fisherman were on the floor of the arena, in an area set off to one side of the weighing platform. They each were swinging their rods in pendular, underhand motions to pitch weighted lures toward a pair of paper cups taped horizontally to the floor 40 feet away. Two out of three times the lures hit the cups on the fly. A few people stood around watching, and listening to Moseley talk about the reel's characteristics without missing a beat in his rhythmic casting. Watching them cast into the cups taped to the concrete was a little sad, like watching gunfighters retired to a wild west show.

During a break, Moseley came to the side and said, "This is all right. I like talking to the people, answering questions. But I'd rather be out there fishing." A few minutes later, at two o'clock, workmen came to clear the floor. They reclaimed the casting area and moved its pipe-and-stanchion borders to accommodate the weigh-in. Moseley wandered back through the displays to the ABU-Garcia booth off the floor. The people who were watching him filed toward the stands to watch the weigh-in.

As spectacle, a bass tournament weigh-in leaves much to be desired. There is no ebb and flow of action, no clash of athlete against athlete, no display of breathtaking prowess like a diving catch, a slam dunk, or an intercepted pass. It is not like watching a sporting event at all. It is more like watching a play with many characters. It is an engaging play, because each new character alters the situation in some way, even if he is only eliminating himself as a factor in the final outcome. Sometimes it plods, and sometimes it speeds along. The tension is caused by what may have occurred, or not occurred, offstage, and only when all the characters have made an entrance are the victor and vanquished at last revealed.

From high in the stands, the floor of the UTC arena looked like a carnival midway viewed from atop the Ferris wheel. The stands descended in terraces of blue and orange from the shadows at the edges of the metal-girdered ceiling, in ever-tightening rings toward the lighted floor. On the floor were the booths and displays, in rows like carnival games, and at one end, where the lights were brightest, the weigh-in. At 2:38 p.m., while the first returning boats were still in traffic, a booming voice announced, "Now, your host for this afternoon, Mr. Bass himself, Ray Scott...."

Scott strode into the spotlight and mounted the steps to the deck of the boat that was being used as the weighing platform. He was wearing an electric-blue suede sport coat with a B.A.S.S. patch on the breast pocket, jeans, tan cowboy boots, an open white shirt, a silk neckerchief, and his white Stetson. He took the microphone and began warming up the crowd of some 3000. Before the day was out, his visitors would include former president Jimmy Carter, who was outfitted by Scott with a red and white B.A.S.S. cap and put to work weighing fish. Carter shared his duties with test pilot and retired Air Force general Chuck Yeager, who was there to promote AC Delco batteries, one of the B.A.S.S. sponsors. Scott was cool to Carter and warm to Yeager, a preference not entirely explained by the sponsorship or Scott's admiration for Yeager's macho exploits. In fact, Scott was a George Bush Republican. He liked Bush in part because Bush had pushed expansion of a fishing excise tax whose revenues supported sport fishing and improved facilities like launch ramps. He had chaired Bush's Alabama primary campaign in 1980, and welcomed Bush, as vice president, to the Classic weigh-in at Pine Bluff in 1984.

Scott began by reminding the spectators that they were subject to television's prying eye. "Those cameras"—Scott pointed to a raised platform facing him—"are so powerful they can look up at the tallest seat, at the littlest lady, and see whether she shaved her legs. So if you ladies have anything to tighten up, or straighten up, you better go ahead and do it."

The first truck arrived and entered through the large door opposite the weighing platform. The crowd cheered as if Tommy Martin and his press partner were gladiators entering in a chariot pulled by fire-breathing stallions. The tow truck cut a tight, tire-squealing circle to the right and was headed toward the door again when it stopped for Martin and his partner to dismount. Martin weighed in six fish that fell short of 6 pounds, and told Scott that yesterday's leaders had not done well. The next several fishermen received polite applause, but the crowd came alive again when Danny Correia entered the arena.

The day before, Correia had been waiting his turn to leave the water when he had spied three shirtless young men waving at him from the shore. Mike Hodgkins, a construction worker, Dave Tomczyk, a dock loader, and Bobby Davis, a telephone repairman, had driven all night from Massachusetts to cheer Danny on in the Classic. "They musta just got here. They're still sober," Danny said.

Now his three friends formed the core of an enthusiastic cheering section that had added some local recruits. An angler from the federation ranks had never won the Classic, and the prospect of an amateur beating out the pros had great appeal. Danny's nervousness and engaging answers at the news conferences—he had been on the stage again yesterday, as one of the leaders—and his strong first-day showing had inspired a current of feeling that an underdog could win. His rooting section faltered when he pulled just two fish from his live well, but it exploded into yells and war whoops when Danny stood up in the boat and held a struggling fish above his head for the crowd to see. His sharp-featured Latin face was bright with an excited smile.

The fish was big. It weighed 5 pounds, 11 ounces. Correia had caught it on his last cast of the day before making his long run back up Nickajack Lake to the frighteningly punctual lock. The smaller fish tacked on a pound, and Danny moved into the Classic lead with a two-day weight of 15 pounds, 3 ounces.

"I knew after practice he was going to do well," said Bob Perkins, vice president of the Massachusetts federation chapter and part of Danny's cheering section. "He's just a machine out there. He's smooth. He's always a contender." His voice contained a note of native pride.

But other fishermen were coming to the stand. Roland Martin appeared with just two fish that weighed 2 pounds and 5 ounces, and dropped back in the pack. "I'll get 'em tomorrow," he promised.

Randy Blaukat moved up two places with three small fish, and Clunn dropped to thirty-first with a single 12-ounce bass. "What's the deal here?" Blaukat wondered. "My hero is crumbling before my eyes. Coffee drinking is doing it to him." Blaukat had learned that Clunn was reading *Eat to Win,* a performance-diet book that

Blaukat, at Shauna's suggestion, also was reading. When he had seen Clunn at breakfast drinking a cup of coffee, he had expressed shock that Clunn was not following as strict a regimen as he was. Blaukat also was surprised when he saw Clunn and Gerri dancing at one of the banquets. "It's strange to see him dancing," he said. In fact, almost anything Clunn did would have sobered Blaukat in some way, because Clunn had the impossible burden of meeting in the flesh the expectations Blaukat had imposed upon an icon.

Jerry Rhyne, a short, burly North Carolina fisherman who ran the Hungry Fisherman restaurant chain's tournament tour, moved into first place at the end of the day with a 6-pound, 14-ounce catch. He was more than a pound ahead, but only 12 ounces separated Danny, in second, and the next three fishermen. Only one, a Classic rookie named Charlie Reed, from Broken Bow, Oklahoma, had caught a seven-fish limit both days. Reed, at 51 the tournament's oldest fisherman, was sitting in fourth place.

Riding in the bus from the arena back to the hotel and convention center, Correia kept glancing sideways and shaping his face into an expression of euphoric disbelief. "Whooooh," he breathed softly, pulling his cap down over his face. He would hide under it for a second or two, and then peek out again, still disbelieving. But after Rhyne, at the news conference, suggested that Danny's knees would be knocking during Saturday's final day of competition, Danny said he didn't expect to need knee braces. "I'm not as nervous as Jerry says I am," he told a questioner. Then he amended his answer. "I probably am. I'm just trying to convince myself I'm not."

He said his plan for the tournament had been to make the top ten the first day and the top five the second. "The third day, I don't think you need any explanation for that," he said.

Correia was growing practiced at the news conferences, but he had not learned to reckon with the B.A.S.S. camera crew that had tracked him down and began shooting him fishing at a few minutes before ten that morning. The crew had rigged him with a wireless microphone, and Danny had returned to fishing. Finally the crew began calling questions to him across the water. "I didn't know you were supposed to say anything," he said. At about ten-thirty, on a day that was producing few strikes—he said he had

only four all day—he missed hooking a fish because he was paying attention to the camera crew.

After that, given the paucity of strikes, Correia had asked his
press partner not to fish. Leo Prince, the outdoor editor of the
Kingston, Ontario, *Whig-Standard,* was an enthusiastic angler, and
he complained to tournament director Sharp at the end of the
day. Sharp used the news conference to remind the fishermen that
they were not supposed to discourage the press anglers. His remarks drew a low "Boooo" from Clunn.

Clunn was among the fishermen most vocally opposed to letting the outdoor writers fish at the Classic, both because he found
their questions distracting and because some fished to beat the
pros. "Take a Randy Blaukat," Clunn said. "If a writer caught a
6-pound fish instead of him, that could be his whole career. If a
writer and not me had caught a 6-pound fish at my first Classic, I
wouldn't be here like I am today."

Clunn's objections were more than hypothetical. It turned out
that on the lake that day his press partner, Gene Mueller of *The
Washington Times,* had more than doubled Clunn's weight with a
1-pound, 10-ounce bass. It was the biggest press bass of the day,
and Clunn was in a snit.

That night, at the Ranger banquet, Jimmy Houston and Roland
Martin were among the fishermen who stopped by Correia's table
to congratulate him on his showing. His room telephone rang late
into the night, and he answered it, "Classic Hotline."

Clunn was more than 12 pounds behind the leader, and Gerri considered it a foregone conclusion that he had no chance to win as
the Classic entered its final day. "I think he can finish well," she
said. "But Ricky is not a notoriously big-fish fisherman."

He still was treated like a star as he rolled toward the launch
ramp on the morning of August 16, sitting on the boat seat with
one foot curled underneath him. A thousand people had gathered to watch the takeoffs. The fishing paparazzi were out in force,
and Clunn lifted his cap to show his face to the blinking cameras.
People thrust caps and programs at him. "Ricky, look here, Ricky,"
a woman demanded, and he looked. "Smile, Ricky," and he smiled.
"Can I have your autograph?" "Sign my cap." "I want to shake
your hand. Any man who can catch seventy-five pounds of bass

(as Clunn had in the 1984 Classic), I want to shake his hand."
Clunn accommodated as many as he could, and then the boat was
in the water.

Waiting for his seven-fifteen start, Clunn tied on a spinnerbait,
a buzz bait, and a "Baby N" crankbait by Bill Norman. He sharpened the hooks of the Baby N with a small file. The lake was
smooth, its surface muddled as if stirred gently from below. A haze
smudged the horizon, and insubstantial clouds gave the sky a cast
of palest pink.

"This thing's not over yet," said Clunn grimly. "I know it's a
cliché, but in this tournament that's really true."

Ray Scott waved his cowboy hat, and the line of boats surged
forward, forging paths of gray through the pink reflection in the
water. Clunn gunned his boat north, and kept going past the river
channels near Harrison Bay where he had practiced. The steam-
shrouded towers of the Sequoyah nuclear plant loomed and then
were left behind. The sun was a red-rimmed orange spot beyond
the haze. Looping clouds of mist, twisted like strands of dough,
hung above the water. A strange flotilla of ski boats, all identical,
passed in the opposite direction. A man and a boy were fishing
from a boat at the edge of the river; the boy's orange life jacket
was startling in the dim color of the morning, like a bright piece
of wreckage on the sea.

Thirty-four miles from the start, Clunn entered a wooded creek
mouth on the left side of the river. He swung the boat's wheel left
and right, and the boat tilted and slipped through a series of tight
curves. Then the trees at the water's edge gave way, and the creek
opened into a broad pool that forked in two directions and was
bordered with houses and meadows. The place was called Mud
Creek, and Clunn went to work. He started fishing near the point
of the peninsula that split the water into its two arms, alternating
between the buzz bait and the spinnerbait and casting with both
hands on the long-handled rods. At 8:29, he boated his first keeper, a 14-inch bass that had taken the spinnerbait.

Clunn worked along the eastward-running arm of the creek,
covering the shallow north bank over the patchy forest of low
milfoil that could be seen beneath the surface. He picked up the
rod with the crankbait and began switching among all three. On
cast after cast of the small crankbait, he reeled in feisty fish no

longer than a rich man's cigar. Successive casts produced two small bass of identical size, and Clunn said, "I think I've caught that one about forty-three times since yesterday," when he started fishing in the creek. But he was convinced the pool harbored big fish, too. The buzz bait formed a torpedolike bulge under the surface as he reeled it in. "I'm trying to get a big one here," he said. "I'm only looking for one strike on that thing."

The houses were substantial, but not lavish. Well-tended lawns descended flatly to the water's edge from backyard decks with colorful umbrellas. Willow, oak, maple, and elm trees stood ranked along the water. Behind one house, a launching ramp intersected the plane of a low seawall. At 9:15, Clunn caught his second keeper, and at 9:40, his third, on the Baby N. Both fish were small.

The thin, vaporous clouds disappeared into the rising heat, and an atmosphere of sullen calm replaced them. The hum of the trolling motor, the chirping of cicadas, and the splash of Clunn's baits hitting the water were the only sounds. Then a raucous flock of geese passed overhead, and a small plane began practicing take-offs and landings at a nearby airstrip. Clunn hooked the fourth bass long enough to keep at 10:42. He stepped to the edge of the boat, stuck his rod tip in the water, and reeled in the fish. He said it was a way to keep the fish from jumping and throwing the hook, and also to keep the crankbait's second treble hook "slapped against his face" to lessen the chance of losing the fish if the forward hook disengaged.

Clunn fished without pausing, working the edges of both arms of the creek, and using the Baby N more than the larger baits in the clear, gray-green water. He was trying to catch a limit before concentrating on catching a "kicker," the larger fish that would boost his catch weight. He stopped long enough to dunk a small towel in the water and place it inside his cap, to cover the back of his dark, leathery neck, where the skin was creased like a turkey's comb. He kept his long sleeves rolled down, and in his dark slacks fished doggedly, casting, casting, casting, now and then bringing in a fish long enough to measure before resignedly throwing it back. Occasionally he took a sip of water. At 12:45, he caught his fifth small keeper.

Clunn fished relentlessly until, at four casts after 1:45, he laid down his rod. He stepped down from the casting deck and climbed into the driver's seat, shrugged on his life vest, and drove out of Mud Creek. Stopping to replenish the boat's gas tanks, he said he felt "numb, indifferent." He stopped for a few last spinnerbait casts, and a few with a plastic worm into the milfoil along the main river channel. They were to no avail, and he turned toward the finish. Streaming toward their congregating point, the tournament boats bounced over rough water, and their wakes flowed like the tails of cantering horses.

The fishermen waited in the cut by the Chicamauga Marina for their tow trucks to arrive and pull them from the water. Gary Klein arrived in Denny Brauer's boat; Klein had lost his propeller shaft and transferred with his fish to Brauer's boat after marking the fish by clipping their belly fins. One of the live wells in Clunn's boat was free, so Klein moved the fish again and rode to the weigh-in with Clunn. Two of the fish were of good size, over 3 pounds each. Klein explained excitedly how he had caught them, curling his hands around an imaginary rod and shaking them as if fighting a bass.

Klein had started the day in seventh place, less than 3 pounds from the lead. "I thought that I could win if I got three hits, and they were the right hits," he said. "And I did.... I got two good hits. I mean, the third one's not bad, 'cause it's a better-than-average fish, but if it would have been the class of the other two, there would be no doubt. And if I'd had another fifteen minutes, I might have caught one more keeper."

Clunn said he thought that 10 ounces would separate the top four places. Klein moved to yet another boat outside the arena, and Clunn gave his friend a clenched-fist sign of support.

Waiting in line to enter the weigh-in, Clunn was besieged with more requests for autographs and pictures. "Rick, look,..." "One more time, Rick."

Inside the arena, Klein's fish weighed 8 pounds and 2 ounces and moved him into the lead. But the top five fishermen were being held back until last, and it seemed unlikely that his margin would survive.

At four o'clock, Scott glanced at a cue card, stared into a camera, and said, "The BASS Masters Classic will be right back." For the first time in B.A.S.S. history, a weigh-in was pausing for commercial time-outs. When the weigh-in resumed, the trim, gray-bearded fisherman from Oklahoma, Charlie Reed, produced his third limit of seven fish and moved past Klein into the lead. Now only Woo Daves from Chester, Virginia, Correia, and Rhyne waited in the wings. Daves had four fish that gave him a total weight of 22 pounds and 8 ounces, ahead of Klein but short of Reed's 23-9. The grapevine gave Rhyne just four small keepers. Danny could win if he matched his first day's performance.

The cheers of 5000 people rose to the ceiling girders when Danny entered the arena. He was the candidate of youth, of the underdog, of dreams come true. The heroes all had failed; Roland Martin, Clunn, Klein, Tommy Martin, Larry Nixon, Jimmy Houston, Orlando Wilson were settled in the middle of the pack with their mediocre fates decided for this day. A Yankee kid from Massachusetts could upset them all. His friend and fishing buddy Peter Emerson had driven all night from Norton, Massachusetts, to be there. The two had come south once before, when they entered a B.A.S.S. tournament at Lake Eufala, Alabama, in 1981. "We were gonna mop 'em up, show those southern boys how to fish," Danny said. "Roland Martin won it, big time. We each caught a fish. That was the first time."

This time, Danny reached into his live well and began pulling out fish. An expectant rustling moved through the hatbox-shaped arena, punctuated by whistles and applause. A shout rang out: "C'mon, Danny." Ray Scott said, "If he can pull a limit out, he may do it. He can win this tournament with eight pounds, seven ounces of bass." Danny reached into the live well six times, and placed six fish in his bag to carry to the platform. Scott eyed his bag and said, "I don't know if he can do it or not."

Danny, on the platform, said to Scott, "I've got six fish here. A couple of them are small ones. I'll just hope for the best."

"All right, watch the scales," said Scott. The arena held its breath. Scott's voice and the large red numbers on the scale display were simultaneous: "Seven pounds, nine ounces." He had fallen 13 ounces short of Reed. The crowd, which had wanted to explode, applauded without joy. On the sidelines, Bill Sisson of *Soundings* magazine, Danny's press partner, said Danny had lost a 3-pound fish.

*     *     *

The news conference postmortem focused on Reed. His wife, Vojai, had won the Bass 'N Gal Classic in 1984, they exercised together every morning, and he planned to keep tournament fishing "until I'm seventy-five. As long as I can stand in the front of the boat, I'm going to be there." The TVA had sprayed the patch of milfoil where he had found his fish, and they had moved, but he'd found them again. He had fished with a plum-colored plastic worm, and after catching a limit on the final day switched to a DB-3 crankbait and improved his weight by culling four fish. He was the only fisherman to catch a limit all three days.

Reed won $50,000, a prize that for a change did not include boats or vehicles. He could also expect to add to his list of paying sponsors, which on the afternoon of his victory included only Ranger Boats. Sponsorships, endorsements, and public appearances could eventually swell the worth of his Classic victory to better than a million dollars.

Correia's second-place finish was the best a federation "amateur" had ever managed in the Classic. He won $13,000, including a $1000 bonus for his big bass on the second day, and stood upon a good launching pad for the professional career he envisioned. Someone asked him at the news conference if he had lost any fish that might have won it. "One," he said. "I had a good fish on but I couldn't get him out of the milfoil." He paused, and with perfect timing added, "I'd like to think it was a carp."

Later, people who had been to many Classics agreed that for perhaps the first time, they would remember who came in second. Correia's effects were far-reaching. By that final news conference, the fishermen who spoke were referring to the small fish they threw back not as "nonkeepers," but as "shorts."

Blaukat, who Danny thanked at the news conference for suggesting the spot in Chicamauga where he caught his biggest fish on the last day, had weighed in one 14-ounce bass and duplicated his regular-season finish of thirty-third. Clunn, his hero, ended up in twenty-sixth.

That night, after the Classic's closing banquet, Correia sat in the lounge at the Holiday Inn, surrounded by his friends from the Massachusetts federation. He sat facing the door, and he looked dazed and happy as he accepted a constant stream of congratulations shouted over the sounds of the band across the room, and dozens of competing conversations. Blaukat collapsed in bed after calling Shauna and his parents. He said he felt "geeked out."

Clunn and Gerri packed for an early departure. They would return home to prepare for Rick's fortieth birthday party, which had been postponed from July 24 so that he could keep his mind on fishing. For Clunn, the tournament had proved a mystery. "I felt good about it," he said. "I never did feel really bad about it, even when I wasn't doing well. I'm not sure where I miscalculated so badly. Even if we had to start over I'm not sure what I'd do differently. The Classic's funny. You're either way out of it or right in it. I was way out of it."

At the hotel, all the talk in the lounge was of the aftermath of the Classic, and everybody seemed to be wearing the blue shirts Ranger had given away. Moseley left the hotel with the men from ABU-Garcia and two other young fishermen who had given casting demonstrations. In the blue neon light of the BeBop Cafe he sipped a Coca-Cola and watched couples dance and watch themselves in mirrored walls. At one o'clock, the crowd began to dwindle. The Brainerd Beach Club was losing its energy too. Moseley's group split up and went its separate ways. Downtown at Yesterday's, young people were four deep at the bar and standing outside on the sidewalk. It was perfect. At last, Moseley was just another young man at the bar, and not a fisherman who had nothing to say about the Classic.

# A New Season

Luminarias cast a festive glow around Clunn's living room and on the spacious deck outside. Shiny Mylar balloons were moored to plants and chairs. The dining table was heaped high with Mexican food. The daylong rain had stopped, and some of the guests were moving outside, balancing plates of food and margaritas or Tecate beers. The luminarias were part of the Mexican theme; Gerri, who wore white for the party, had cut the sides of some of the bright paper bags, flickering with the light of the candles inside, to read "Ole!" Others read "40." One read "Old Fart." It was September 6, and Clunn was celebrating his birthday, six weeks late.

It was surprising how few of the guests were fishermen. Mike Dyess, the good-humored part-owner of Stanley Jigs and a Montgomery resident, was there. So was Rick's cousin, Randy Fite, who was dark, bearded, and quiet. Clunn and Fite called each other brothers, because Rick's father had taken in his sister's children when she and her husband were killed in an automobile crash. Raised in the same household, though they were seven years apart, the two had developed a strong bond. Fite joined the B.A.S.S. tour three years after Clunn, and had fished six Classics. In the final hours of the U.S. Open, Fite had kept his boat close to Clunn's to make sure he could return for the weigh-in. And moon-faced Billy Murray, who paid Clunn $450 a day to conduct continuing-education seminars on bass fishing, was there as well. But the rest of the thirty or so guests were family and friends apart from fishing: Gerri's parents, the Montgomery County district attorney, an airline pilot, an elementary school teacher, a contractor, an artist, a management instructor; the sort of people and professions of which communities are made.

After the party had moved outside onto the deck still wet from the rain, two large women arrived. They wore exotic clothing—a peacock feather tiara, clinging gowns, black undergarments. Their names were Ruby and Marlene, from Hippogram, and they looked carefully at Clunn as if they remembered him from somewhere. One declared she was his high school girlfriend.

"I'm sure I would have remembered that," Clunn said.

The Hippogram women's routine was predictably ribald, and after they had left, Clunn opened his presents. They were predictable, too, having to do with fishing, turning 40, or Clunn's libation of choice, W. L. Weller whiskey. He read each card, and displayed each present, even the de rigueur bottle of Geritol.

The party wound down and the guests drove away into the night, and Clunn and Gerri and their houseguests repaired to the hot tub set in a corner of the deck. The Texas night was full of stars and everyone was mellow. The ethereal music of Vangelis played over loudspeakers hidden in the eaves. Sitting in the pulsing, steaming water, Clunn extended his legs and poked his toes above the surface. He contemplated them for a moment, wiggled them, and said, "You all stick your toes out of the water." Three more sets of toes appeared. "Look at them. Now, can you tell if there's really any connection between your body and your mind?" Nobody could form an answer.

After the Classic, Clunn lay fallow for a while. He celebrated his birthday, and stayed around the house. Days after Brooke and Cortney returned to school, he put on khakis and safety glasses and climbed on his small blue Ford tractor to mow the coarse meadow grass around the lake. Clunn was not particularly handy. Gerri said, "Rick can take a car that's not running right and work on it for two hours, and it won't be running at all." But he liked the mowing; it was peaceful and finite and orderly, and it connected him to the 38 acres of gently contoured meadow and pine and pin oak woodland in a way that renewed his strength and clarity of mind. He whacked at the weeds sprouting around the brick posts—an American flag flew from one, and the flag of Texas from the other—at the entrance to his property, replenished the deer feeder hidden in the trees, and took pleasure in the land and in the small lake he had had built in front of the house and stocked with Florida bass.

He and Gerri had bought the land in 1979, installed rail fencing, and dug the lake. Then the demise of *The Southern Outdoorsman* television show, which Clunn had hosted, reduced his income by $30,000 a year, and they postponed building the house. The two-story, stone-and-frame contemporary, shaped like an open "L," was completed in June 1985. Its 1800-square-foot deck alone was larger than the house they left behind.

The deck extended over the lake, and Clunn hung fishing rods from hooks outside the door. When he felt restless, he grabbed a rod and cast from the edge of the deck. If he didn't catch anything after a cast or two, he hung up the rod again and went on to something else. He would shoot baskets with Brooke and Cortney at the basketball hoop out by the garage (Brooke played for her junior high school team), or swim with them in the lake, or he and Gerri would ride their bicycles around the country roads outside Montgomery. Sometimes he did nothing at all but lie on the bed and watch football and baseball on television.

Clunn displayed his trophies in his large upstairs office, which overlooked the living room and the lake beyond the windows. B.A.S.S. plaques and plaques from the Pasadena, Texas, bass club were arrayed on the walls. A couple of dusty mounted bass had yet to find a place, and lay on the floor against the wall, next to a rack of lake maps. The large facsimile check for $100,000 from Operation Bass, for his win in the Red Man All-American, hung over his desk above an IBM personal computer. Clunn tried to find the time before each tournament to look up the results of previous tournaments held during the same season of the year. It helped him establish the pattern and lures most likely to win the tournament. Now he was entering the same data into the computer, and at the touch of a button would be able to produce a printout with the twenty years of information it had taken days of reading to recall. With such records, Clunn could bypass unproductive water. He knew where the fish were most likely to be, and what lures and techniques were most effective.

Clunn's fishing library, including *Rick Clunn's World Championship Bass Fishing*, which had gone to three printings, and a fishing board game he'd endorsed as "the closest thing to real fishing I've ever experienced," occupied shelves near the door of the office. (Gerri described the game, "Lunker," as "an unfortunate investment.") Clunn's library of mental exploration was closer to hand, on his wall-length desk next to the computer.

There were the books his contemporaries found so strange, for which they labeled him "Conehead" Clunn. *The Portable Thoreau, The Writings of Ralph Waldo Emerson*, Whitman's *Leaves of Grass*, and Einstein's *Ideas and Opinions* were lined up with *Agartha, A Journey to the Stars, Kundalini Yoga for the West*, and Shirley MacLaine's *Out on a Limb*. His bookshelf contained *Meditation and the Mind of Man*, based on Edgar Cayce readings, *Flight of the Seventh Moon*, and *Medicine Woman. The Poetry of Robert Frost* stood next to *The Resurrection of the Body* and down a few books from Plato's *Dialogues* and *Coming Back: The Science of Reincarnation*.

Sitting at his desk on the weekend of the party, leaning back in his creaking wooden desk chair as a ceiling fan hummed overhead, Clunn had said, "All of it adds. It's amazing, the interconnectedness of it all.

"You go back to Plato, and he was saying the same thing that Whitman was saying, and any of the great minds. They're all saying the same thing. Even Einstein. There's that intuitive part of us that's there, trying to tell us something. Your imagination is your link to God. That's your creative ability."

He sipped on a cup of after-dinner coffee, and a cuckoo clock piped out the hour, eleven o'clock.

Fishing, Clunn said, was only the backdrop, the vehicle for his pathfinding. Fishing "allowed me to break through," he said. "But I'm getting where now I feel so deeply about this mental stuff that I care almost as much about it as I do about my fishing. I apply it to fishing because it's such a beautiful, pure laboratory for it. I've always known—and if you read Whitman and Emerson, they'll tell you that everybody should feel this—that my connection is to those trees and those woods and nature and everything that's around me. I can go out there and feel what I always felt as a kid and never could describe and didn't understand."

Clunn repeated his plan to seek a new consistency in the tournament season ahead. He was serving notice that he would halt most of the promotions and college seminars for which he was paid handsomely, up to $15,000 in a year, but which took him away from home for as much as two and three months out of twelve. "The most unjust a father can be is being a tournament fisherman," he had said at the U.S. Open. He believed that fewer distractions would not only allow him to spend more time at home but help him fish well enough to make up the loss in income. He refused to say he was going to shoot for Angler of the Year, but you got the feeling that he was.

"I want to step all my tournaments up several levels as far as my intensity, my concentration, my performance," he said. "Even the most insignificant tournament, I've got to take it more seriously. If I only allow myself one or two motivated events a year, I'm cheating myself. Why don't I make every day a search for these answers? The more I work at it, the quicker I'll get to where I'm going. I believe I can get to the level where I'll win forty or fifty percent of the events that I fish.

"Obviously if I accomplish that, I should win Angler of the Year, or be awfully damn close to it."

The season opened on the Hudson River at the small town of Catskill, New York, on October 1. Randy Moseley, Randy Blaukat, and Danny Correia checked into the Rainbow Cabins on the Saturday before the tournament for three days of official practice, and shoehorned themselves and three friends into a two-bedroom trailer. Sleeping comfortably was difficult, but it was cheap that way.

Moseley was stretching his money. He had found a sponsor, an electrical supply house in St. Louis that had agreed to provide him $6000 in expenses in return for half his winnings for the year.

Moseley anticipated a modest income from his ABU-Garcia contract. "Every cent counts," he said of the $100-per-month agreement. He said he had signed on as teaching pro staff editor for a small newsprint magazine, *The Midwestern Outdoorsman,* for another

$100 a month. Bumblebee Baits was selling his spinnerbait, the one he had used at MegaBucks with the oversized blades, and had agreed to pay Moseley 3¢ per bait sold.

"I've got myself into all kinds of things, really," Moseley said, sitting in the dining room of the Friar Tuck Inn on the night before the tournament. "But they just haven't all come together." He had seen no money, and had so far signed no contracts cementing any of these deals. "I need to do that, I guess. I probably should, but I just don't know, really, how to go about it."

But Moseley was upbeat. He felt the breaks were starting to go his way. He was being asked to do occasional seminars. Ranger Boats was continuing to pay his B.A.S.S. entry fees, one tournament at a time, and that encouraged him. "I'm so confident right now," he said. "I'm more confident now than I think I've ever been, just because of the way things are coming together." His voice simmered with enthusiasm as he talked about the fish he had found in practice. "Only twice before have I felt like I had something that could win a tournament, and once was at MegaBucks," he said. "Well, the third's right here. I was shaking all morning this morning. I'm excited. I'm on some good fish."

He leaned forward earnestly to say he had found three spots for big fish and two for keepers, "bank runners, I call 'em. Between those five spots, hopefully I can catch a limit every day that'll weigh fourteen, fifteen pounds, and take a shot at winning this thing."

By contrast, Clunn was unhappy with his practice. He had come off the water early, disgusted with himself, and stood beside his boat drinking a wine cooler with Gary Klein as they basked in the warm fall afternoon outside his cabin at Carl's Rip Van Winkle Motor Lodge. A young fan Clunn had invited to fish with him had just left with his father, and another father brought another son to meet Clunn and Klein and get their autographs.

"I made a nondecision today," Clunn said when they had left. Strands of gray hair were beginning to show above his temples. "I went upriver because of the wind coming upriver against the tide. By the time I changed my mind, it was too late."

Later, after the pairings were announced and Moseley had persuaded his partner to go in Moseley's boat to Moseley's fishing spot, Clunn agreed to ride with New York angler Dick Garlock.

*        *        *

On the morning of October 1, a new moon rode in the early darkness and stars shone between the clouds. The light rose, and the tournament boats assembled in Catskill Creek and drifted slowly on a falling tide. Clouds drifted from west to east, and the trees showed the red-gold blush of fall. Leaves fluttered from the trees into the water, and eddied in the boat wakes. It was the beginning of a painful day.

That afternoon, two fishermen were returning downriver to the weigh-in, and a third, who already had weighed-in, was traveling north on the river to his docking site. The two boats collided as the drivers attempted to avoid each other. Leslie Foster, 65, the driver of the northbound boat, suffered a fractured hip. Jimmy Atkinson, a 37-year-old touring pro from Lorena, Texas, and 36-year-old Daniel Barragan of Little Falls, New York, were killed.

Gerri Clunn, staying with friends in New York City while Rick fished the tournament, heard the news on the B.A.S.S. call-in tournament hotline. She blanched and put her hand over her mouth as if she was going to be sick, and sank into a chair. Atkinson and his wife (they had two teenage children) had been friends of the Clunns, but it was more than that. It was the unspoken fear she felt each time Rick left for a tournament, each time he went out on the water, the fear that for all of his caution and competence anything could happen.

"As we get older, I fear a little for his physical well-being," she had said. "I want him to stay healthy. He can't do what he's doing if he isn't healthy."

The accident recalled what a tenuous life the fishermen led, how close to the edge most of them were financially and physically. Mercury had just begun providing its national team members on the circuit, including Atkinson, with major medical health insurance; and life insurance that paid $60,000 in case of accidents. But the price of independence for the majority of the fishermen was a lack of the benefits, like comprehensive life and health insurance, that most corporate employees took for granted. There was no workers' compensation, and no disability insurance. And on every lake and river lay the potential for disaster, in the form of the elements, inexperienced or impaired boat drivers, or, as on the Hudson, a simple, fatal miscalculation that led two experienced drivers to continue at full speed and turn toward each other and not away as they tried to avoid a collision.

Atkinson and Barragan were the first contestants to die on the water in the history of B.A.S.S. tournaments. A New York State Troopers' report assigned no blame. Investigator James Mills called it a case of driver error and said, "This was simply a tragic accident." Harold Sharp said that in every tournament, "it's always a relief when everybody's back."

Two days later, another Texan, David Fenton, won the tournament with 49 pounds and 2 ounces of bass.

Randy Moseley finished tenth, his best performance since Mega-Bucks. His 34 pounds, 5 ounces of bass won $2100 and put him on a fast track for the Classic. Gary Klein had said, "You don't make the Classic in the last tournament. You make it in the first one."

Clunn, acting the contrarian, finished thirty-second with 27 pounds, 13 ounces. He said he had lost the tournament in practice, by refusing to fish the creeks entering the river, where most other fishermen had found their bass. "I knew they were in there," he said. "I just didn't want to go in there where everybody was."

Moseley left immediately after the weigh-in for the airport at Albany and a flight to Kentucky, where he would fish a Red Man regional tournament he hoped would carry him to the All-American. A friend he had brought with him would return to Missouri with his boat.

"I've got my transmission in overdrive, and I'm just going to keep going full-speed," Moseley said. "I'm lookin' for a good year. Finally."

Moseley failed to make the All-American. Construction began on the house at Sunrise Beach on the shore of Lake of the Ozarks. Jean put her Great Aunt Jo's bequest into the down payment and the furnishings, and they figured their payments would be just a little more than the $315 they were paying for rent. In November, Randy moved Jean and Justin to Clewiston, Florida, where he would spend the winter guiding on Lake Okeechobee out of Roland Martin's Clewiston Marina. They lived in one room of a house shared with other fishermen, and Randy guided almost every day.

The season's second tournament was held on Lake Okeechobee, and Randy finished a disappointing 155th after losing a big
fish that "straightened out a 4-aught hook like it was a bobby pin."
He reckoned it would have gone at least 10 pounds. He also did
poorly in the third tournament, on West Point Lake between Georgia and Alabama, where he finished 157th.

Meanwhile, his financial problems seemed to have no end. His
van broke down again, and his four-wheel-drive Cherokee had
problems, too. The memo bills for his boat and motor came due,
and since he still had not sold his boat, he was unable to pay them.
When he found a buyer, he could not give the boat up because he
needed it for guiding. A new boat awaited him, but he failed to
pick it up and it was sold. Randy borrowed a car to tow his boat to
Leesburg for MegaBucks, the first tournament of the new year.

There, Randy's partner on the third day accused him of cheating by deliberately snagging a fish, a violation of the tournament
rule that says fish must be caught in a "conventional and sporting
manner." Randy vehemently denied the charge. Faced with a choice
between throwing the fish back and taking a lie detector test, he
offered to take the test. But when he learned he would have to
travel to B.A.S.S. headquarters, which he had neither the time nor
money for, he chose to throw the fish back. B.A.S.S. tournament
officials were satisfied, and other fishermen said they were behind
him, but Moseley kept hearing tales about himself—"ninety percent of it bad"—and it depressed him. "I feel let down by my
friends," he said.

As winter turned to spring, Jean packed to go home to Missouri and Randy conducted his last guide trip of the winter on
Lake Okeechobee. The invitational tournaments that led to the
Classic and Angler of the Year resumed at the Sam Rayburn Reservoir in Texas during the last week in March. Moseley had slipped
to forty-seventh in the Classic standings, but he still had a taste of
confidence, his old elixir. He vowed, "I'll kill 'em at Sam Rayburn."

The second half of the B.A.S.S. season began without Harold
Sharp. He resigned after seventeen years with B.A.S.S. and went
to work for Orlando Wilson. Wilson, on his way to another Classic appearance, was ever the entrepreneur. He signed several fishermen to exclusive contracts to do instructional videotapes. As a
result, he squabbled with B.A.S.S. over its tournament release
form, which gave the organization carte blanche use of the video

shot during tournaments. Ray Scott looked back on the twenty
years of B.A.S.S. and delivered nostalgia a swift kick. "I enjoy
thinking about the good old, bad old days, but I don't want to go
back to them," he said. "Sure, it's less informal now. But that's
progress."

*The BASSMASTERS* began its second season on the Nashville
Network, and featured Randy Blaukat as a struggling pro. Blaukat
ranked 167th entering the season's second half. While he de-
spaired about making the Classic, he and his partners were taking
Ultra Tournament Products public for an infusion of capital that
would allow them to expand, and he began a series of weekly fishing tips for a Joplin television station. After the tournament at
Sam Rayburn, and the next at Lake Guntersville in Alabama at
the end of April, Blaukat had improved his standing to seventy-
third. But with just two fishing days that counted in the Super-
Invitational at Kentucky and Barkley Lakes near Paris, Tennessee, at the end of May, the Classic was out of reach.

Danny Correia ranked 126th in the Classic race after the Guntersville tournament. He worried that people would think his 1986 Classic performance was a fluke, but he picked up Ranger Boats and
Johnson outboards as memo bill sponsors. Joe Thomas and Rich
Tauber ranked forty-first and forty-seventh, respectively, in the Classic standings, and Thomas went on to make the 1987 Classic.

Moseley did not "kill 'em" at Sam Rayburn. Fair showings at Lake
Guntersville and in the Super-Invitational left him out of the Classic
for another year. But by then Moseley had shaken off the depression he felt after MegaBucks. He was buoyed by wide-ranging expressions of support. Ray Scott, who admired Moseley's flamboyance,
dismissed the incident. He said, "Show me a guy who doesn't see
some controversy, and I'll show you a colorless man."

Moseley found new sponsors who would stake him to another
year, gambling on a portion of his winnings. He invested $750 in
shares in Randy Blaukat's company. One early summer morning,
he confided on the telephone that he was toying with "some new
ideas, advertising ideas, that I want to approach some major companies with, if I can just get in touch with the right people."

As for the year ahead, he said, he was more confident than ever.

Clunn, after finishing seventh on Lake Okeechobee and fifth
at West Point Lake, made the MegaBucks finals and finished

eighth. He crept within $12,000 of Roland Martin's $297,420 at the top of the B.A.S.S. all-time money-winning list. He moved into the traditional strong point of his season ranked second in the race for Angler of the Year.

A lackluster performance at Sam Rayburn dropped him to fifth. In April, Clunn returned with the other fishermen to Lake Guntersville, site of his first Classic victory in 1976, and won the tournament with a 42-pound, 6-ounce catch. He moved into first place in Angler of the Year by a slim 2-pound margin with two fishing days to go. And he finally passed Martin, his arch-rival. His $30,000 prize put him first on the B.A.S.S. all-time money list, $317,708 to Martin's $304,820.

Clunn's triumph was sweet, but it was brief. He lost the Angler of the Year title to Denny Brauer in the season-ending Super-Invitational. In seventeen days of fishing from September through May, he had landed 160 pounds and 7 ounces of bass to Brauer's 161 pounds, 11 ounces, a difference of a single fish. Though Clunn finished a respectable twentieth in the tournament, Larry Nixon finished second and became the leading B.A.S.S. money winner.

Clunn made an effort to be philosophical. All he had ever wanted, he said, was to be consistent. He had stunk it up at Sam Rayburn, he said, and didn't deserve to win. But yes, he was a little disappointed. More than a little, actually.

"It kind of burned me that I didn't win it, just to be honest about it," he said over a humming long-distance line after the season was over. "But being that close, I think, has made me more determined. I didn't really have that burning desire to win it until I lost it."

He looked forward to another year in which to seek perfection. And the U.S. Open and the Classic, after all, were coming up again.

Late at night on the weekend of his birthday, Clunn had pondered a question. Given his moodiness, his preference for solitude, his efforts to shut out all distractions, the esoteric books he read, in spite of his success what did other fishermen really think of him?

Clunn's mouth widened in a smile. "I think I keep surprising them," he said. "I think I've surpassed what they expected, and now it's like they can't really figure out what I'm going to do next."